Praise for The Best Yes

"In a loud and shouty Internet age with more people than ever before vying for our time and attention, learning how to say 'no' is a survival skill. One that we women especially need help mastering. Setting healthy boundaries without giving up on community altogether is the biblical life skill that Lysa unpacks with grace, faith, and a great sense of humor in this book. Reading it was like remembering how to exhale."

—LISA-JO BAKER, BEST-SELLING AUTHOR OF *SURPRISED BY MOTHERHOOD: EVERYTHING I NEVER EXPECTED ABOUT BEING A MOM* AND COMMUNITY MANAGER FOR THE WEBSITE INCOURAGE.ME

"Lysa's pen is vibrant, her heart pulsates with understanding and warmth, and her yeses are wisdom-sharp. I'm tired of tired. This tome of truth arrived in the nick of time. Thanks, Lysa. I needed to get back on track with my Best Yeses and kind noes."

—PATSY CLAIRMONT, AUTHOR OF *TWIRL: A FRESH SPIN AT LIFE*

"I love *The Best Yes*! Wise, warm, honest, funny, and do-it-now practical, this guide to making smart decisions is just the thing for those of us who have too much on our calendars and need help to stop the madness. Lysa has clearly lived and learned what works and what doesn't. Her stories, examples, and advice all ring true, and wisdom pours from every page. This is her best yet!"

—LIZ CURTIS HIGGS, BEST-SELLING AUTHOR OF *BAD GIRLS OF THE BIBLE*

"*The Best Yes* is Lysa at her best: warm, wise, practical, honest. This topic is so timely for me, and for every other busy woman and mom I know, and Lysa has both instructed and inspired me through these wonderful and necessary pages."

—SHAUNA NIEQUIST, AUTHOR OF *BREAD & WINE*

"Like few other women I know, Lysa has the ability to move us from a stuck place to a place of freedom. If you, like me, have spent much of your life saying 'yes' to things you wish you had the courage to say 'no' to, this book will be a game changer. It's a book you will want, not just for yourself but for all the women in your life. When we understand the scriptural principles outlined here, then every 'Yes!' will be intentional, significant, and whole-hearted. Thank you, Lysa!"

—SHEILA WALSH, AUTHOR OF *THE STORM INSIDE*

"The biblical filters in *The Best Yes* are amazing tools to better process my thoughts and actions. With Lysa's help, the Bible is beginning to speak personally to me."

—JILL W.

"A MUST read. And then MUST read again! FABULOUS book!!!"

— NICCI R.

"*The Best Yes* poignantly talks about the struggle between our hearts and our heads as we try to live up to the world's Super Woman challenges for our lives. This book is helping me break the cycle of stress, exhaustion, and overcommitment from trying to please everyone."

—SUSAN D.

"One of the best time management books ever! Not only does this book help you to prioritize your schedule, but it takes the Word of God and teaches you how to apply it to your daily life. Then you can make choices that honor God and see where you are truly called to be."

—LORI B.

"*The Best Yes* is a life changer for women trying to cope with the demands of frazzled, unfulfilled living. Lysa gives practical and godly insight for wisely choosing the Best Yes in order to restore balance and bring joy back to everyday life."

—MELANIE P.

"It was like a pep talk straight from God through Lysa to my own spirit! Chock-full of insight and practical application, this book will change the way you look at God's plan for you and how to be a part of it! I could read it again and again and again!"

—WENDIE C.

"Lysa has already taught me how to watch what goes into my mouth and wait before letting words come out of my mouth (in her books *Made to Crave* and *Unglued*). Now she is teaching me how to watch what goes into my spirit, so that I can wait on the Holy Spirit and give my Best Yes in all circumstances. I'm in awe of how God is using *The Best Yes* to help me be an OVERCOMER."

—SHELLY C.

"Thank you so much for this book. It has brought tears to my eyes and laughter in the bad days. It has given me the words I was thinking, but could not speak. I think this book should be in the hands of every woman in a position of leadership in the church and for sure in the hands of all women to empower them to give their Best Yes."

—ROBYN C.

The Best Yes

MAKING WISE DECISIONS IN THE
MIDST OF ENDLESS DEMANDS

Lysa TerKeurst

NELSON
BOOKS

An Imprint of Thomas Nelson

Published in Nashville, Tennessee, by Nelson Books, an imprint of Thomas Nelson. Nelson Books and Thomas Nelson are registered trademarks of HarperCollins Christian Publishing, Inc.

Published in association with the literary agency of Fedd & Company, Inc., Post Office Box 341973, Austin, Texas 78734.

Thomas Nelson titles may be purchased in bulk for educational, business, fund-raising, or sales promotional use. For information, please e-mail SpecialMarkets@ThomasNelson.com.

Unless otherwise noted, Scripture quotations are taken from the Holy Bible, New International Version®, NIV®. Copyright © 1973, 1978, 1984, 2011 by Biblica, Inc.™ Used by permission of Zondervan. All rights reserved worldwide. www.zondervan.com.

Scriptures marked AB are from THE AMPLIFIED BIBLE: OLD TESTAMENT. © 1962, 1964 by Zondervan (used by permission); and from THE AMPLIFIED BIBLE: NEW TESTAMENT. © 1958 by the Lockman Foundation (used by permission).

Scriptures marked MSG are from *The Message* by Eugene H. Peterson. © 1993, 1994, 1995, 1996, 2000. Used by permission of NavPress Publishing Group. All rights reserved.

Scriptures marked NKJV are from THE NEW KING JAMES VERSION. © 1982 by Thomas Nelson, Inc. Used by permission. All rights reserved.

Scriptures marked ESV are from THE ENGLISH STANDARD VERSION. © 2001 by Crossway Bibles, a division of Good News Publishers.

Scriptures marked HCSB are from HOLMAN CHRISTIAN STANDARD BIBLE. © 1999, 2000, 2002, 2003 by Broadman and Holman Publishers. All rights reserved.

Scriptures marked NLT are from *Holy Bible*, New Living Translation. © 1996. Used by permission of Tyndale House Publishers, Inc., Wheaton, Illinois 60189. All rights reserved.

Library of Congress Cataloging-in-Publication Data

TerKeurst, Lysa.
  The best yes : making wise decisions in the midst of endless demands / Lysa TerKeurst.
    pages cm
  Includes bibliographical references and index.
  ISBN 978-1-4002-0585-1
  1. Decision making—Religious aspects—Christianity. 2. Choice (Psychology)—Religious aspects—Christianity. 3. Time management—Religious aspects—Christianity. I. Title.
  BV4509.5.T45 2014
    248.4—dc23   2014003582

Printed in the United States of America

15 16 17 18 RRD 12 11 10 9 8

Contents

Chapter 1

Check the Third Box

DRIVE-THRU ORDERING AND MY YOUNGEST DAUGHTER are a bad combination. Brooke can do many things in life. She's an amazing, beautiful, talented, witty, kind-hearted girl. Who is amazing. I believe I might have mentioned that already. But she panics at the drive-thru box.

Even if we've talked about getting her order in mind beforehand, something always goes haywire. She takes way too long to give me her order. She changes things even after I start placing her order. She confuses the poor order taker who isn't making enough money per hour to deal with people like us.

I feel so awful, like we are breaking drive-thru rules. I know we're aggravating the people behind us. The cars aren't honking, but I can feel their stares and glares and the desire for us to hurry up. The tension mounts to where I know a honk is coming any minute now, I just know it is. I'd pull out of line and circle back around if I could, but you can't at this drive-thru.

There are poles in the ground to keep traffic flowing correctly, so once you commit to going through this drive-thru line, you are committed. Even if your daughter can't decide. Even if the line behind you now is wrapping around the building. Even if the order taker is secretly wishing you'd go away. You can't. I can't. We can't.

I sweat. And start smelling like onions. The kind of onion smell coming from a deodorant fail. Seriously. All from our drive-thru order taking too long.

I keep saying the next time it happens I'm going to look straight at her with all the love a mama tired of smelling like onions can muster up and say, "Give me your order now or I'm leaving." Just tell the girl at the box we are so sorry but we have no order so we'll be circling around to the place where we can pull out of line and then leave.

Just pull away.

Drive her home to eat dreaded leftovers. Or toast. Or nothing. Because she's got to learn this lesson!

And here's the thing that really baffles me—the drive-thru restaurant we go to most often? Her dad runs it. As in, she's been going to this place her whole life. From day one in utero she's been nourished by the homemade goods from this eating establishment. And the choices of menu items? She likes just about everything at this restaurant. I've seen her eat and enjoy many, many things on the menu. So I know that no matter what she chooses, she'll enjoy her meal.

But still she's paralyzed when it's time to order.

Why?

Because she doesn't want to pull away from that drive-thru, get a few miles down the road and a few bites into her meal and wish she'd made a different choice. It's not that she'll think what she ordered is bad, it's just that she'll feel the tension of realizing she missed the best choice. And we girls don't like feeling we missed out. Or messed up. Or misstepped right out of what should have been or what could have been.

༄

As I think about that frantic drive-thru frustration from her not being able to make a decision, I am challenged to be honest about my own struggles with decisions.

I exhale and some unfiltered honesty rushes in.

I struggle with decisions too. I don't want to miss out on opportunities, mess up relationships by disappointing people, or misstep right out of God's will. I struggle with keeping some sense of balance in my life. I struggle with worrying about what others think of my decisions. I struggle with wondering if my inability to do it all will make my kids wind up on a therapist's couch one day. I struggle with feeling like I can't quite figure out how other women seem to do it all. I struggle with feeling like I'm going to let God down. Descriptions ping in my head: *I'm tired. I'm distracted. I'm disappointed in myself. I feel slightly used and more than slightly used up. I'm a little overwhelmed and a lot worn down.*

These are thoughts I share only with myself. Partly because I'm a positive person and these threads of admission feel too dark. And I much prefer cheery yellow to gloomy gray. Also I hesitate to share because I can't figure out how to fix these things, so why even bring them up? In the daily sea of endless demands, I must admit I'm not doing so well. So I put pen to paper and dare to explore this topic as an author who needs this message most of all.

This time is hard for me. Admission instead of omission.

Admitting that I sometimes need to reevaluate. A few minutes to whisper, "God, I really want to do life right. So I give and serve and love and do and sacrifice. I do it all with a happy heart, an open checkbook, a calendar dedicated to being Your girl. I study Your Word. I tuck truth in my heart and as a trembling, brave one, I determine to charge upward and forward each day."

And yet there's this nagging sense that something's a bit off inside me. Someone makes a request of me that I know right away is unrealistic. My brain says no. My schedule says no. My reality says no. But my heart says yes! Then my mouth betrays my intention of saying no, as it smiles and says, "Yes, of course."

I dread saying yes but feel powerless to say no. I dread saying yes not because I don't love that person. I love them very much. But I dread what saying yes will do to the already-running-on-empty me.

And I keep on marching as if this is the way a Christian woman is supposed to live, as if this is the call on my life, as if this is all there is.

I misuse the two most powerful words, *yes* and *no*. I slap purpose across the face and stomp calling into the ground as I blindly live at the mercy of the requests of others that come my way each day. Every assignment feels like my assignment.

You need me? You got me. Because I'm too scared or too cowardly or too busy or too *something* to just be honest and say, "I can't this time."

In this great day when most women wave banners of authenticity about our pasts, we crouch back from honesty about our presents. We'll tell you all about our broken places of yesterday but don't dare admit the limitations of our today.

All the while the acid of overactivity eats holes in our souls. And from those holes leaks the cry of the unfulfilled calling that never quite happened. We said yes to so much that we missed what I call our "Best Yes" assignments—simply because we didn't heed the warning of the whispers within that subtle space.

I'm tired. I'm distracted. I'm disappointed in myself. I feel slightly used and more than slightly used up. I'm a little overwhelmed and a lot worn down.

We must not confuse the command to love with the disease to please. And it's not just because of the vicious cycles of people pleasing, although that's part of it. I miss Best Yes opportunities sometimes because I simply don't know they're part of the equation. I get all twisted up in making the decision to check either the Yes or No box, not realizing there is a third box that reads Best Yes.

We must not confuse the command to love with the disease to please.

What is a Best Yes, you ask. We'll unpack this throughout the book. But in its most basic form, a Best Yes is you playing your part.

At church.

At school.

At work.

At wherever you are today.

And what's so great about that? In God's plan, you've got a part to play. If you know it and believe it, you'll live it. You'll live your life making decisions with the Best Yes as your best filter. You'll be a grand display of God's Word lived out. Your undistracted love will make your faith ring true. Your wisdom will help you make decisions that will still be good tomorrow. And you'll be alive and present for all of it.

A Best Yes is you playing your part. If you know it and believe it, you'll live it.

Are you ready to begin asking, *What is my Best Yes?*

Me too. I just need to wrap up this little situation at the drive-thru first. Any suggestions for a stronger deodorant? I have a feeling I'm going to need that.

Chapter 2

The Way of the Best Yes

LAST CHRISTMAS I WAS DISTRACTED AS I OFTEN AM DUR-
ing the holidays. Every year I say I'm going to get better about
scaling back so I can really keep my focus where it needs to be
for the season. I have moments where I do this well. But I have
other moments that are just plain pitiful.

Honestly, I can be an utter nincompoop.

I was rushing about, frustrated. I went to Target for wrapping paper and somehow left the store having spent ninety-
seven dollars on who knows what. Then got all the way home
before I realized I left the wrapping paper on that little shelf
underneath the shopping cart. At checkout I didn't remember to
grab it and purchase it. So all my moments of trying to match
this and that to keep up with expectations in this Pinterest-
crazed world were all for nothing.

Now I'd be using recycled Happy Birthday bags—wrinkled
and well past their prime—for the gifts that needed to be

wrapped right this second or we were going to be late for the Christmas party. And then—oh my, glory heavens—I remembered I was supposed to bring cookies to said party.

A–M last names were supposed to bring appetizers.

N–Z last names were supposed to bring desserts.

Desperation found me digging in my pantry, emerging with some Easter chocolates shaped like eggs and wrapped in pastel foil. *I'll call them chocolate ornaments,* I rationalized.

While all this was happening, my husband, Art, kept saying something to me about wanting to give money to one of his employees.

"We'll have to talk about that later," I snapped back, aggravated that he thought this moment of rushed panic was a good time to bring up giving. My brain went off on this tangent of thoughts about how I give and give and give and give and sometimes just get sick and tired of giving. So now I'm bringing Easter candy to a Christmas party I don't even want to go to with presents wrapped in birthday-balloon-covered bags.

"Mom, why did you wrap the gifts that way?" The teenager with her hand on her hip had no clue how close I was to seriously canceling Christmas. Not just this party. But the whole December 25 situation.

"Oh, you don't even know the half of it. We're also bringing Easter candy for our dessert. And if you say one critical comment about my obviously brilliant party-attending skills, we won't go. You hear me? Not one more word. Now go get in the car, and let's pretend like we're happy to be going to this party."

And then my husband said something else about not being able to wait to talk about the money needed to help his employee, and I snapped back once again, "I don't want to help."

You know that wonderful feeling of conviction that says without a doubt you are the worst human on the planet? Like if they were handing out certificates for "worst person," you would own the title for this moment in history? That would have been my moment.

I was so caught up in the rush of superficial things in my world that I missed hearing the cries for help in someone else's world. God had been prompting me to listen, really listen, to my husband, to stop and focus and give him just a few minutes. But I refused. I rushed past. And I acted like I was perfectly justified in doing so.

My husband was requesting money for a precious family I hadn't met yet. The wife had just started working in the kitchen at my husband's restaurant. They were from another country and didn't speak English. This made it difficult to let others know about their need for help. They didn't have many friends here. And they had just been through the most tragic event of their lives. They'd had a daughter born in late spring with many complications. And just that morning she'd lost the battle for her life.

While I was stressed about leaving my wrapping paper at Target, a friend of this mom called my husband to ask for help to pay for a funeral.

When I finally clued in to what my husband was talking about, I felt so horribly convicted. It wasn't just about being too busy, it was also about my closed-fisted reaction when I knew he wanted to talk about giving money.

I can just be so flat-out rebellious sometimes.

Just that morning I'd been praying and asking God to show Himself to me. I asked the God of the universe to intersect my life with His revelation, then got up from my prayers and forgot to look. Forgot to seek Him. Forgot to keep my heart in tune with His voice and His invitation.

All because of the chaotic rush of my day.

When all of life feels like an urgent rush from one demand to another, we become forgetful. We forget simple things like where we put our car keys or that one crucial ingredient for dinner when we run into the grocery store. But even more disturbing, we forget God. We say with our mouths that we are trusting and relying on God, but are we really?

A quick check to see if this is true is our ability to notice what God wants us to notice and our willingness to participate when God invites us to participate.

DON'T MISS YOUR ASSIGNMENT

I have to admit, I rush and miss God's invitations a lot. I walked by a woman at church today with pale skin and a bald head. A quick stirring in my heart said, *Go say hi.* I brushed it off.

I saw a discarded cup in the parking lot of the restaurant where I had lunch. I knew I was supposed to pick it up and throw it away. I walked right by it.

For two weeks now I have felt this prodding to have my daughter's friends over for a special dinner and Bible study night. I have yet to talk to her about it or set a date.

These were all simple acts of obedience I missed. But not missed because I was unaware. They were missed because I was busy—caught in the rush of endless demands. And the rush makes us rebellious. I knew what to do and blatantly ignored it.

Ignoring God's leading doesn't seem like such a big deal in these cases. In the grand scheme of the world, how big a thing is it that I didn't pick up that cup? After all, how can I be sure it was really God?

I think a better question would be, *How can I be sure it wasn't God?*

If we are to be Best Yes girls, we have to long for unbroken companionship with God. The cup was a little deal unless it was me breaking away from obeying His instruction. The one who obeys God's instruction for today will develop a keen awareness of His direction for tomorrow. I'm always asking God for direction, but I'll miss it if I constantly ignore His instruction.

The one who obeys God's instruction for today will develop a keen awareness of His direction for tomorrow.

It's in those little breaks in our companionship with God where confusion sets in about what we're really supposed to do. Remember in chapter 1 where I said we must not confuse the command to love with the disease to please? Not being able to hear God's direction is the exact spot where this confusion gets so many of us in trouble.

Have you ever heard that amazing verse from Isaiah that says, "Whether you turn to the right or to the left, your ears will hear a voice behind you, saying, 'This is the way; walk in it'" (30:21)?

I love this verse! I want it to be true for me! I want my ears to hear God say, "This is the way; walk in it."

I want that with every fiber of my being. Don't you? Can you imagine how much angst and pain we could save ourselves if we were really that in tune with God?

It is possible. But there's a process involved. Let's consider that verse within its historical context. In verses 15–18, God is speaking sternly to the leaders of Israel for turning to Egypt and other pagan nations as military alliances instead of seeking His help:

> This is what the Sovereign LORD, the Holy One of Israel,
>   says:

> "In repentance and rest is your salvation,
>   in quietness and trust is your strength,
>   but you would have none of it.
> You said, 'No, we will flee on horses.'
>   Therefore you will flee!
> You said, 'We will ride off on swift horses.'
>   Therefore your pursuers will be swift!
> A thousand will flee
>   at the threat of one;
> at the threat of five
>   you will all flee away,
> till you are left
>   like a flagstaff on a mountaintop,
>   like a banner on a hill."

> Yet the LORD longs to be gracious to you;
>   therefore he will rise up to show you compassion.

For the LORD is a God of justice.
  Blessed are all who wait for him! (30:15–18)

Right here the Amplified Bible adds *blessed* are those "who [earnestly] wait for Him, who expect *and* look *and* long for Him [for His victory, His favor, His love, His peace, His joy, and His matchless, unbroken companionship]!" (v. 18). Who doesn't love that? You'll notice a shift in tone here as the verses continue because God is speaking to the general population of Israel:

> People of Zion, who live in Jerusalem, you will weep no more. How gracious he will be when you cry for help! As soon as he hears, he will answer you. Although the Lord gives you the bread of adversity and the water of affliction, your teachers will be hidden no more; with your own eyes you will see them. Whether you turn to the right or to the left, your ears will hear a voice behind you, saying, "This is the way; walk in it." Then you will desecrate your idols overlaid with silver and your images covered with gold; you will throw them away like a menstrual cloth and say to them, "Away with you!" (vv. 19–22)

This is how God is speaking to me through these scriptures because I can identify with both audiences. Most of us are leaders in some capacity and followers as well.

- God asks us to return and rest.
- But we say no and speed on our own course.
  (Remember the rush can often make us rebellious.)
- The Lord is gracious and shows us loving-kindness even while we run ourselves ragged.
- He hears our cries. He answers with compassion.

✦ Yes, there are consequences for our refusal to listen, but there's always a second chance to experience that unbroken companionship when we wait expectantly for Him—or, as the Amplified Bible says, when we look and long for Him.

✦ So He whispers, "Say hi to her; pick up that cup; have those girls over for dinner. Look for Me. Long for Me. Experience unbroken companionship with Me."

✦ Then we will see and hear Him.

✦ And these other idols we're so bent on chasing—anything we prioritize over God—we'll be able to let them go.

Do I do this perfectly? Obviously not. I missed three chances today already. There was a fourth chance I didn't miss, a Best Yes that didn't fly by me unaware. But it only came after I whispered, "Forgive me." I'm making the choice to stop the rush, to notice, and to obey.

Then God gave me a do-over.

I remembered the woman I rushed by at church. I felt a stirring to track her down through a mutual friend and send a simple e-mail. Just a small note. Which I sent. For no other reason than God saying, "This touch is one of your Best Yes assignments for today. Don't miss it."

That e-mail paved the road for me to have coffee with this woman. During that coffee, God gave me an answer to something I'd been begging Him to speak to me about. I thought I was going to help her and I was the one helped. Obeying God's instruction definitely led to me being able to discern His direction. I needed that coffee meeting, and it never would have happened had I not stopped the rush of my life and sent the e-mail to the woman God had prompted me to connect with.

That little act of obedience somehow unplugged my spiritual ears. Not that we can't hear God otherwise. But hearing Him clearly? I think that might require my soul to acknowledge what all my rushing causes me to miss.

ℒ

If we want to hear from the Lord, we must confess that sometimes we walk right past the Lord's instruction and set ourselves up to miss His direction. If we want His direction for our decisions, the great cravings of our souls must not only be the big moments of assignment. They must also be the seemingly small instructions in the most ordinary of moments when God points His Spirit finger saying, Go there. And in doing that, we are companions of God with eyes and ears more open, more able, more in tune with Him.

Back to my Christmas story. My focus was more on pleasing the people of that party than being present with my own family. It was all about keeping up appearances rather than staying connected to God. That night I asked Art and the Lord to forgive me. And Art wrote the check to help pay for the funeral.

SEEK INSTRUCTION BEFORE DIRECTION

A few days later we walked into the small church service. The cries of the mother draped over the tiny white casket up front made my breath catch in my throat.

We sat in the back. The mom's best friend ushered her from the casket to the front row. Then the service started. Everything was spoken in a language we didn't understand.

If we want His direction for our decisions, the great cravings of our souls must not only be the big moments of assignment. They must also be the seemingly small instructions in the most ordinary of moments when God points His Spirit finger saying, Go there.

But we didn't need words to have our hearts closely in tune with the sadness of the moment.

The mom whispered to her friend something that made her turn around. She looked at us. She got up in the middle of the preacher's message and made her way back to where we were seated. She motioned for us to follow her.

I didn't understand. I felt the red-hot flush of eyes on us when they should have been focused on the purpose of this moment. Not us. We were just supposed to be part of the small audience. We weren't supposed to be walking up the aisle in the middle of this family's most private and tear-filled moment.

The friend pointed for us to sit in the front row with the mom and dad. It felt like an honor we didn't at all deserve.

Then the pastor asked for the interpreter to come forward. This next part of the service would be spoken in two languages—their tongue and ours.

"You have given our family, our community, a gift in being able to have this service today," the pastor said. "And while we will never be able to pay you back in money, we want you to know we are committed to paying you back in prayers for your family. Little Emily was born on May 26 and lived a short but important life . . ."

He shared more but I don't remember the rest. My mind swirled in utter shock. It was as if God were whispering, "Remember—pay attention—see what I want you to see." That morning, before going to the funeral, I'd written out very specific prayers for my daughter Ashley. I then asked God to please show me some confirmation that He'd heard me. Then in the middle of a funeral, God gave me the gift of this whole community praying for my family.

Prayers that I hardly deserved.

Prayers from people who in the midst of their own pain were willing to give.

Prayers that were so much more valuable than the cheap money we'd given. Cheap, cheap money.

And then, just to make sure I knew—absolutely knew—that this was one of those divine moments from God, little Emily and my Ashley shared the same birthday, May 26.

With all my heart, I wish this story was one where Emily would have been born well and healthy, a story where God's divine intervention meant that this family wouldn't have needed a funeral. But this broken world gives broken stories. And that's just what this is.

Still, in the midst of it all, God is there, pointing us toward unbroken companionship. My mind was stunned by just how gracious God is. By how much He wants us to pay attention to His instruction so He can reveal His direction.

Don't miss this. Unbroken companionship helps us hear His instruction so then we can see His direction. We must not seek direction before obeying His instruction.

Let's bend our knees in repentance first. Let's not forget to capture the small opportunities to keep that unbroken companionship. For it's in the midst of them where we hear His voice behind us saying, "This is the way."

The way of the Best Yes.

And once we know, believe, and start to live the way of the Best Yes, then we're ready for a little bit more. That soul thing you dream about and that wakes you up in the middle of the night? That calling? That assignment? The one you say, "Pick me, God! Pick me!" Yes, let's go there next.

Chapter 3

Overwhelmed Schedule, Underwhelmed Soul

I'VE GOT TO BECOME A FEARLESS FOSBURY.

Now, before you read any further, y'all know I'm not a sports girl. But I am a story girl. If you want me to watch ESPN with you, you better hope it's one of those nights when they are featuring stories about athletes' lives, families, and obstacles they've had to overcome to get to where they are. All that stuff keeps me interested. And will keep me from driving you crazy with dumb questions and crazy observations about how out-of-fashion many of the uniforms are these days and if they'd only add a little style, blah, blah, blah.

Gracious, where were we? Oh yes, I'm not a sports girl. Right. But I found this story about an athlete who changed his approach and what a difference it made. He was a high jumper named Dick Fosbury, and he caught my attention because my daughter Ashley's sport of choice is pole vaulting, which is similar to the high jump—but we'll talk more about that later.

For now, let me just be completely legit and honest about where and how I found this story—on a TV commercial while trying to turn the channels past the sports stuff. I was headed to HGTV but got a little turned around. And then this commercial about a man who flipped convention on its head grabbed me. Not because I liked the Mazda6 it was promoting. No, it was the grainy, black-and-white image of a man doing things differently.

With the traditional approach to the high jump, an athlete could only go so high. But Fosbury had the crazy idea of going higher by lowering his center of gravity. All he had to do was go headfirst and backward. That's why they called him Fearless. Using the new technique—which used to frighten his coaches— Fosbury set an Olympic record. Of course, he never could have done that with the old technique. He had to change his approach if he wanted to improve his abilities. So he did just that.[1]

He tried a new technique. He established new patterns. He changed his approach. And not only did he gain the highest level of success in doing all these things, he transformed the sport. Today, more than forty years later, jumpers are still using the Fosbury technique. What if we, like Fosbury, decided to flip our current decision-making technique?

Here's the reality of our current technique: Other people's requests dictate the decisions we make. We become slaves to others' demands when we let our time become dictated by requests. We will live reactive lives instead of proactive.

And reactive lives get very exhausting, very quickly. We get requests. We fill up our schedules all the way to the limit. We leave very little white space. We live lives that exhaust us.

We never change our approach. Therefore, we never experience the thrill of that deep soul satisfaction.

If I want things about my life to change, if I want to change the way I use the world's two most powerful words, *yes* and *no,* it won't happen just by trying harder or dreaming more or even working myself to death. I have to change my approach to the way I make decisions. The same patterns will produce the same habits. The same habits will lead to the same decisions. The same decisions will keep me stuck. And I don't want to be stuck.

I want to become a Fearless Fosbury.

HOW WE SPEND OUR SOULS

A woman who lives with the stress of an overwhelmed schedule will often ache with the sadness of an underwhelmed soul. An underwhelmed soul is one who knows there is more God made her to do. She longs to do that thing she wakes up in the middle of the night thinking about. Each January she writes on her resolutions list to get started on that thing this year.

A woman who lives with the stress of an overwhelmed schedule will often ache with the sadness of an underwhelmed soul.

Her thing might be to . . .

- Write a book
- Run a backyard Bible club for neighborhood kids
- Go on a mission trip
- Own a small bakery
- Go back to complete her degree
- Turn her photography hobby into a business
- Teach a class at her church
- Get out of debt
- Work with a local ministry

But then the next January comes. And the next. And the next. And still that thing is relegated to the bottom of the list. If it even makes it on the list. Maybe the only time for it is those middle-of-the-night thoughts tangled in the blur between sleeping and not. Or those precious few quiet moments in the shower. But the time to actually spring those things into action seems to evaporate as quickly as the steam from the shower. And then it's just another day. With another list. And time just marches on without ever seeing her thing come into being.

What if we dared to take time to write out that new height or next big goal for our lives? The thing we want but never really plan for.

And then what if we were honest enough with ourselves to actually write down the first steps for accomplishing that thing? And then what if we were audacious enough to actually schedule time to work on those first steps? Please reread that last sentence very carefully. That's right. Schedule time to work on those first steps for this thing I'll call our soul thing.

The decisions we make dictate the schedules we keep. The schedules we keep determine the lives we live. The lives we live determine how we spend our souls. So, this isn't just about finding time. This is about honoring God with the time we have.

Remember in the last chapter we talked about unbroken companionship with Jesus? The small ways come first. But then there's this soul thing. This getting more intentional with how we spend our souls is also part of the unbroken companionship with our Lord. It's a new way of being intentional with playing the part God wants us to play.

It's not that how we've been living is bad—just like Fosbury's old jumping method wasn't a bad method. He still cleared the bar. But he dreamed of more, higher heights. And I suspect that's true for you too. Dick Fosbury discovered his new heights in being able to jump over his obstacle by turning his body so that his back went over before his feet.

That's an interesting concept to me.

He literally backed in to his jump.

And when I think about the changes we need to make so our thing doesn't keep getting crowded out, I think we may have to back in to it as well. Instead of waiting for the time to get started to simply appear one day, we need to be intentional with scheduling it.

My thing for years was the desire to write a book. Honestly, I'd probably still be dreaming about doing this had I not learned the reality of the number 3.5.

I'll explain why 3.5 is such an important number in just a minute. But first we have to start with another number—168. This is the number of hours God entrusts me with each week. No more. No less.

Don't start having flashbacks from Mr. Murphy's math class and tune me out. I promise we're going somewhere with this exercise. Somewhere more than that horrible math word problem about two trains leaving the station traveling different rates in different time zones carrying different loads. My brain has a painful throb just thinking about that kind of math. So, no, we're not going there.

We're going to do an "hours assessment" of our weeks. Your list of tasks may look very different from mine, but you can at least use my list to get thinking about yours. (To take your own personal time assessment, go to TheBestYes.com.) Here are the tasks that are pretty common and consistent with the realities of my life responsibilities and the ones I could track the number of hours required:

Sleeping
Meals
Quiet time
Family time
Ministry prep work
Church serving and attending
Date night
Time with friends
Exercise
Meetings for Proverbs 31 Ministries
Errands and household responsibilities
Kids' activities and other scheduled events

When I add up all those numbers, they total 164.5 hours. What's left of the 168 hours in a week is only 3.5 hours. And we all know that 3.5 hours can get eaten up very quickly by just a few requests. And most of us are getting more than a few requests each week. It's no wonder we live with overwhelmed schedules and underwhelmed souls.

I've felt that ache. When I've let my schedule get out of control, it's my soul that suffers the most. Other things suffer for sure. My family time. My attitude. My stress level. But the deep sadness in my soul is the hardest of all to shake.

Unless we get incredibly intentional with the 3.5 hours we have left, they will simply and tragically leak away. Of course your number will be different from mine, but the principle is the same. How we treat our hours will be very telling in whether or not we'll ever become Fearless Fosburys.

Back to my desire to write a book. I never "got around to it." And I never "found time for it." Then, how are you holding in your hands book number seventeen that I've written? Because I figured out that trying to "get around to writing" or "finding extra time to write" never worked for me. I had to work my schedule to accommodate my writing.

I literally blocked out those 3.5 hours I just mentioned. I took control of those hours. I grabbed them before anyone else could. I dedicated those hours each week to that thing I knew God had woven into the DNA of my heart.

I remember the first time I had to decline a friend's invitation to meet at the restaurant with the indoor playground because I'd scheduled writing time. I felt so foolish. I wasn't a writer to her. Shoot, I wasn't a writer to myself either. I'd never written anything of any kind of significance—unless you count that little book of poems I'd made for my mom when I was ten, the one with the poems written on parchment paper with burned edges. I was totally into burned edges back then.

I wasn't a writer by anyone else's account except my mother's. But she was also the one who told me I could be a country singer because I had the voice of a honky-tonk angel. This kind of motherly love is exactly what gets people their fifteen seconds of shame on those TV singing shows. Moms, I love you, but please don't encourage your babies to sing when they can't sing.

No, I couldn't sing. And maybe I couldn't write either. A book of poems written as a child hardly proved any sort of talent or ability. But writing was in my soul. And it had to come out. I knew it.

At this point I was just a girl who talked about wanting to write. And now I had to decline my friend's invitation because on my little paper calendar I'd written from noon to 3:30 p.m. "writing time." Everything in me wanted to just cross out that ridiculous 3.5-hour scheduled writing appointment and go eat fries in the midst of colored plastic tubes and screaming kids.

I stood at my white linoleum countertop with the cordless phone receiver in my hand staring at my calendar. It was my Dick Fosbury moment. Was I going to just go with what felt normal to me that day and meet my friends for lunch? Keep the familiar steps? Do what others wanted? Stay within the bounds of the expected?

Or would I dare to turn my body? Go over the bar backward? Keep my writing appointment? Dare to put pen to paper? Honor God with this gift He'd given me for stringing words together?

And completely change my approach to those 3.5 hours—hours that on previous weeks just leaked away from me?

God had given me a gift of this time.

My time. My choice. My approach.

Your time. Your choice. Your approach.

What's that soul thing for you, that God-honoring thing that keeps slipping away because there's been no time to set aside and actually start? What's your number? Take your 3.5 and schedule the start of your thing right now. It's your Dick Fosbury moment. It's time to set your soul free from being chained to an overwhelming schedule.

After all, remember the decisions you make determine the schedule you keep. The schedule you keep determines the life you live. And how you live your life determines how you spend your soul. Those 3.5 hours seem like a reasonable gift to give to your soul right now.

Yikes, I hear the critics' brakes screeching right here. Right now. They are jumping out of their criticism caravan holding up posters with these verses on them:

> Do nothing out of selfish ambition or vain conceit. Rather, in humility value others above yourselves, not looking to your own interests but each of you to the interests of the others. In your relationships with one another, have the same mindset as Christ Jesus: Who, being in very nature God, did not consider equality with God something to be used to his own advantage; rather, he made himself nothing by taking the very nature of a servant, being made in human likeness. (Phil. 2:3–7)

The decisions you make
determine the schedule you
keep. The schedule you keep
determines the life you live.
And how you live your
life determines how you
spend your soul.

The critics would be wrong to use these verses because Paul wasn't talking about personal ambition but about the unity of the church. Though Paul wasn't referencing schedules here, I think it's important to understand this soul thing isn't about us. It isn't about selfish ambitions or vain conceits. It's giving voice to what otherwise just stays a quiet whisper locked inside. It's about letting out that cry of passion God entrusted to you. It's about letting it all the way out so as to touch others, help others, and bless others.

To do this soul thing is actually the exact opposite of selfishness. Keeping it inside with no chance to bless others would be the selfish thing to do. With the right attitude, letting it come to fruition is the only way it can serve others. Interestingly enough, that same chapter of Philippians goes on to remind us not to run or labor in vain:

> Do everything without grumbling or arguing, so that you may become blameless and pure, "children of God without fault in a warped and crooked generation." Then you will shine among them like stars in the sky as you hold firmly to the word of life. And then I will be able to boast on the day of Christ that I did not run or labor in vain. (vv. 14–16)

"Then you will shine" sure sounds like what the soul of a woman fulfilled should resemble. Remember Jesus called us to be a light to this world. When I, with a giving attitude, express that part of my soul literally dying to be expressed, I shine a reflection of Jesus. It isn't about this woman backing away from serving others. It's about finding her way to serve and shine in her Best Yes assignments.

SO THAT I MIGHT BLESS WHOM?

To check my attitude, I've decided to add the phrase "so that I might bless whom?" to the end of my soul-spending activity. Let's look at those activities we listed beforehand:

- ◈ Write a book . . . so that I might bless whom?
- ◈ Run a backyard Bible club for neighborhood kids . . . so that I might bless whom?
- ◈ Go on a mission trip . . . so that I might bless whom?
- ◈ Own a small bakery . . . so that I might bless whom?
- ◈ Go back to complete my degree . . . so that I might bless whom?
- ◈ Turn my photography hobby into a business . . . so that I might bless whom?
- ◈ Teach a class at my church . . . so that I might bless whom?
- ◈ Get out of debt . . . so that I might bless whom?
- ◈ Work with a local ministry . . . so that I might bless whom?

Those 3.5 hours of writing per week have now turned into many years of articles and books. I'm amazed at how crucial that moment was—standing at that white linoleum counter trying to decide between keeping that first writing date or blowing it off and eating fries with my friends. I'm not saying had I missed that one moment I would have never become a writer and let that voice of passion out. But I did just find out about some fruit I would have missed had I not captured saying yes to that moment on that day.

Two weeks ago I saw an amazing answer to this question—so that I might bless whom? I was at a speaking engagement signing books. About ten people into the line, two women approached me holding up a picture of a very handsome young teenaged boy. "He is alive because of your words," they said with big smiles on their faces.

The women looked vaguely familiar, but I couldn't remember how I might know them. They continued:

> Fourteen years ago we knew a little about your story from an article you wrote about the heartbreak of your abortion. My daughter read that article and begged my husband and me to see if we could come talk to you as a family. My husband was a preacher of a small church, and when we found out our young teen daughter was pregnant, the shame felt overwhelming. We couldn't process any other way out than for her to have an abortion. But then we found your words. And you agreed to meet with us. We honestly didn't think meeting with you would change our minds. But we were wrong. Through you we saw a hope for how we might choose to honor God through this situation rather than hide in the darkness of our pain and shame. That next week my husband stood before our congregation and told the truth about what our family was facing. He invited my daughter up, and with tears streaming down his face, he invited the congregation to support her, love her, and stand with her as she made this courageous choice to keep this baby.

Tears came to my eyes as I stared at the picture of that baby who had grown up to be that teenaged boy. I hugged both women and something deep in my soul rejoiced. Not for what I'd done—but for what God allowed me to experience through being obedient to Him. Indeed, 3.5 hours had been a terrific way to spend my soul the day I wrote that article. An article that reached far beyond where I ever could have. Into a pastor's family. Into a girl's womb. Into a life saved.

How we spend our souls matters. These are our Dick Fosbury moments. But it's not enough to know that these are moments of decision. We have to desire to become fearless with these moments. Fight through the doubt and discouragement and awkwardness of new. That's why I said I want to become a Fearless Fosbury.

What about you? Don't get so locked in to your overwhelming schedule that you haphazardly spend your soul. It's time to flip that. Never is a woman so fulfilled as when she chooses to underwhelm her schedule so she can let God overwhelm her soul.

Chapter 4

Sometimes I Make It All So Complicated

MY HUSBAND WAS OUT OF TOWN RECENTLY WHEN A BOX was delivered to my doorstep. It was rather large. Not the size of a dresser but definitely larger than the typical package. And it was heavy—too heavy for me to manage alone.

The UPS man graciously brought it inside since it looked like it might rain that afternoon. But I figured it might be a bit much for me to ask him to take it past the foyer, up the stairs, down the hall, and into the room my husband calls his man cave, which is where I like to put things I don't know what else to do with. That would be a long haul, and I could sense this deliveryman's graciousness ended at the foyer.

So there it sat, this mysterious, heavy box.

Deep inside, I knew this was nothing but some product one of my people had ordered. And I knew what to do with it.

Open it. Identify the owner. Tell said owner to figure out a way to get it out of the foyer and into his or her room.

But I didn't listen to that awareness deep inside. I ignored it and listened to my fears instead. You know you've watched one too many mystery TV shows when your first thought about a mysterious box sitting in your foyer is that a person with scary intentions could fit inside. Yes, a crazy person with weapons could mail himself right into your foyer and sit there all day, quietly waiting until you went to bed. And you can hear everyone later watching a reenactment of the unfolding tragedy screaming at you, "Don't leave the box in your foyer! Get it out of the house!"

Ahem. I'm a completely rational person. Except when I'm the opposite of that sometimes.

So I kicked the side of the box to see if there was any kind of reflex action that might happen if there was a living thing inside of it. There wasn't, of course. But then I decided just to be really sure, I would stand around the corner from the box to see if I could step out of its line of sight and possibly hear something: a cough, a slight sneeze, anything.

I was just being sure. Absolutely certain. I could leave no room for doubts, no room at all for any possible bad outcome from this box—a box that I eventually opened with a knife. Just in case. Only to discover a dorm-room refrigerator that one of my people had ordered. Oh, for the complicated love of Pete. I just wasted half my day worrying about a box that contained a dorm fridge.

But we do this sometimes. We do. We have a decision to make and we have that deep-down knowing. We know what to do. We know what the answer is. We do. But we don't go with that knowing. We overprocess the what-ifs and the but-thens and the maybes until we find ourselves standing around a corner listening to see if a cardboard box containing a refrigerator might sneeze.

Good glory.

Now, it goes without saying, there are certainly some decisions that need to be processed. We will spend plenty of time in future chapters discussing how to process decisions that need to be made. But then there are other decisions we just simply need to say yes or no to and move on. Find that courageous yes. Fight for that confident no. Know it. State it. Own it. And move on without all the complication.

Find that courageous yes.
Fight for that confident no.

Do you know what I mean? Sometimes it just comes down to that deep whisper within that says, "Uh-huh, yes." Or a simple, "No, not that."

God has woven into us the ability to discern what is best.

And this is my prayer: that your love may abound more and more in knowledge and depth of insight, so that you may be able to discern *what is best* and may be pure and blameless for the day of Christ. (Phil. 1:9–10, emphasis added)

Discerning what is best is something we're capable of doing as we layer knowledge and depth of insight into our lives. Read those verses again and see that gaining knowledge and depth of insight will allow us to develop a trustworthy discernment.

Knowledge is wisdom that comes from acquiring truth.

Insight is wisdom that comes from living out the truth we acquire.

Discernment is wisdom that comes from the Holy Spirit's reminders of that knowledge and insight.

The Holy Spirit helps us remember that knowledge and insight so we can display it through good judgment in our everyday-life decisions. That's the deep knowing I'm talking about.

WHERE WISDOM GATHERS, NOT SCATTERS

The other day I was talking with a young mom at the gym where we both work out. She was telling me she's really been struggling with the decision of whether to let her two-year-old go to preschool a couple of half days a week next year. As I listened to her, I felt compelled to ask her these three questions:

1. Have you been reading and praying through God's Word lately?
2. Have you been applying God's Word to your mothering lately?
3. Have you sought godly counsel and insights from wise people who know specifics about your situation?

The answer to all three of those simple questions was yes, so I reminded her that she was assigned by God to be this child's mother. If she had done these three things, then she had the ability to discern what was best.

She didn't need to wait for some big neon sign to drop down from heaven to know what to do. If she had that deep knowing this was a no answer for her child, then she should go with that. If she had that deep knowing this was a yes answer for her child, then she should go with that. It's not about trusting ourselves. Rather, it's about trusting the Holy Spirit to do what Jesus promised us: "But the Advocate, the Holy Spirit, whom the Father will send in my name, will teach you all things and will remind you of everything I have said to you" (John 14:26).

When we've done what we need to do to acquire the knowledge and insight of truth, then the discernment of that truth is there. We must learn to trust and use that discernment because the more we do this, the more wisdom we acquire.

Now, here's the flip side of that. When we haven't been doing what we can to acquire knowledge and insight of truth, the discernment of truth probably won't be there. We may have an intuition about something, but intuition and discernment are two very different things.

The definition of *intuition* is a perception of truth independent of any reasoning process.[1] It's based on a gut feeling. But we must be careful just simply going with our gut if we haven't checked it against truth-based knowledge and insight.

Discernment according to our key verse allows us to know what's best—not just have a gut feeling about what's best. Let's read it again:

> And this is my prayer: that your love may abound more and more in knowledge and depth of insight, so that you may be able to discern *what is best* and may be pure and blameless for the day of Christ. (Phil. 1:9–10, emphasis added)

I had another conversation the other day with a girl I know who has been considering making a job change. Her gut said go for it. But when I asked her those same questions I posed to the mom earlier, I got very different answers.

1. Have you been reading and praying through God's Word lately?
2. Have you been applying God's Word in your life lately?
3. Have you sought godly counsel and insights from wise people who know specifics about your situation?

Her Bible had been sitting on her shelf collecting dust for a couple of months. She'd been too tired after going out on Saturday nights to make it to church on Sundays. She'd been gravitating more and more to her party friends rather than her praying friends. So, it was pretty much a no to each of the three questions.

I challenged her to wait to make the decision about a job change until she started developing a truth-based pattern of knowledge and insight. Then she'd have a much better chance at discerning what would be best.

We have to put our hearts and our minds in places where wisdom gathers, not scatters.

The Best Yes is what we're after. Best Yes answers are much more likely to happen when we are in the habit of seeking wisdom. We have to put our hearts and our minds in places where wisdom gathers, not scatters.

Wisdom makes decisions today that will still be good tomorrow. Wisdom gathers at Bible study. Wisdom scatters at the bar. Wisdom gathers when you serve and invest in your local church. Wisdom scatters when you become disconnected from your church family. Wisdom gathers in conversations that are honoring. Wisdom scatters in conversations that are gossipy. Wisdom gathers when my mind is engaged with truth. Wisdom scatters when I watch hours of mindless TV—especially, *ahem*, the kind that leads me to fear that assassins are hiding in refrigerator boxes in my foyer.

Wisdom makes decisions today that will still be good tomorrow.

When a woman uses that powerfully effective combination of knowledge, insight, and discernment, she becomes a wise decision maker. Wisdom is hers. And that's what I want for us. I want us to become powerfully effective decision makers. Because then we will live powerfully effective lives. And spend our souls doing powerfully effective work to the glory of God.

CAUTION—DON'T DESPISE THE DAILY STUFF

But let's not get ahead of ourselves. I realize today might not seem full of powerful options when there are dishes piled in the sink, laundry stinking from being left wet in the washer all night, and dog poop in the corner of the den. Awesome.

Or maybe you are staring at a stack of college loans, final exam notes, and an invitation to your best friend's wedding. The one you are a bridesmaid for and had to spend two hundred dollars you didn't have for a dress you'll never wear again. Despite her assurances you will get lots of re-wear opportunities from this one, you know it will do nothing more than take up space in your already overcrowded closet. And to top it all off, you have no date to the wedding. Awesome.

Or maybe you just got the schedule for the greeter team at church, the team that has to wear T-shirts. Every Sunday. It's your only day to sleep in and make up for the rest you desperately need, and now they are requesting you arrive even earlier this week to help set up for a special luncheon for first-time visitors. Awesome.

You feel all fired up and epic, talking about being powerfully effective. And inside your head a crowd roars with cheers, *Go, girl, go! The world is waiting for your brand of awesomeness. Fulfill your calling. Tell the whole world about Jesus. Rahhh!* And then you look up from the inspiration of these pages and see dog poop.

Life has such a habit of stripping the feelings of power and significance right out of our scope with its constant daily demands. Right?

Let me pull you close and whisper a heart-stopping truth.

That daily stuff—those responsibilities that seem more like distractions—those things we want to rush and just get through to get on with the better and bigger assignments of life—those things that are unnoticed places of service? They are the very experiences from which we unlock the riches of wisdom. We've got to practice wisdom in the everyday places of our lives.

Never despise the mundane. Embrace it. Unwrap it like a gift. And be one of the rare few who looks deeper than just the surface. See something more in the everyday. It's there. We can learn right here, right now, in the midst of all that's daily how to become wise. As we wisely gain knowledge through everyday stuff, grasp insights through everyday stuff, and grapple with the development of our discernment through everyday stuff, we'll use what we have to our advantage in making better decisions.

Like Lucy from the *Peanuts* cartoon, we must get good at using what we have. Lucy once demanded that Linus change TV channels, threatening him with her fist if he didn't.

"What makes you think you can just walk right in here and take over?" asks Linus.

"These five fingers," says Lucy. "Individually they're nothing, but when I curl them together like this into a single unit, they form a weapon that is terrible to behold!"

"Which channel do you want?" asks Linus, relenting. He then looks down at his fingers and says, "Why can't you guys get organized like that?"

Our everyday stuff may seem as ordinary as Lucy's hand having fingers. But when you wisely curl together the knowledge, insight, and discernment formed in your everyday-life experiences, you form patterns of wisdom. Patterns of wisdom will build your confidence to make good decisions, the kind made in the everyday and the epic.

But let's not make Lucy our shining example of this. Heavens no. I suspect Lucy wanted to flip the TV station from some sporting event to the show about the assassin in the refrigerator box. And we all know where that leads.

No, I want to show you this in a biblical woman I just discovered recently, one I now adore. As in, when everyone is lining up in heaven to meet all the famous Marys and Martha and Ruth and Esther, I'm going to rush to a different line. I can't wait to meet this woman only whispered about in a little, tucked-away place in the Bible.

In the midst of King David's great big story, there is a story short on word count but long on impact. It doesn't get a lot of press within the pages of Scripture, lots of details are missing, and I've never, in all my churchgoing years, heard a sermon featuring this story.

We don't know her name or whether or not she had a family.

We don't know the way she earned a living, or whether she wished her thighs were smaller and her arms didn't jiggle when she waved.

We don't know if she was stylish or plain, rich or poor, good with keeping her checkbook balanced or a bit more financially whimsical.

We don't know if she was creative or conservative or contemplative or crazy fun.

And honestly, I like that we don't know all those details. Why? Because it makes it much easier to just slip right into this story and imagine.

Imagine having gained such knowledge, insight, and discernment that the one thing you're known for is wisdom. How do I know she was wise when so much else about her remains a mystery? Because that's the one fact the Bible makes sure we know. Scriptures call her "a wise woman," one who lived in a town that suddenly found itself in quite a bit of trouble (2 Sam. 20:16). A traitor named Sheba was hiding behind the city walls, so King David's fighting men were on the attack.

There was no time to delay, get panicked, or react with anxiety. There was no time to call together the townspeople and have a committee meeting. There was no time to research, study, or kick the box just delivered into her foyer.

She had to trust that her knowledge, insight, and discernment were wise.

> All the troops with Joab came and besieged Sheba in Abel Beth Maakah. They built a siege ramp up to the city, and it stood against the outer fortifications. While they were battering the wall to bring it down, a wise woman called from the city, "Listen! Listen! Tell Joab to come here so I can speak to him." He went toward her, and she asked, "Are you Joab?"
>
> "I am," he answered.
>
> She said, "Listen to what your servant has to say."
>
> "I'm listening," he said. (vv. 15–17)

I have to pause right here and point out something about this woman. We know this woman was wise because the Scriptures label her as a wise woman. But wisdom wasn't just her label; it was also her lifestyle.

Remember, through the stuff of everyday life, if we learn to apply wisdom, we then can own it. Through her everyday life she must have had issues to deal with, problems to figure out, bills and bridesmaid dresses and loans and Linus boys preventing her from watching her favorite channel on the TV.

Yes, certainly she had circumstances. And tangled in those encounters, she learned how to untangle her reactions. She knew how to keep her cool in the midst of a battle. I know she was acting with wisdom rather than wild irrationality because of the response of King David's commander, Joab. He does something he wouldn't have done if this woman were approaching him full of chaos. He went toward her and he listened to her.

No man wants to go toward and listen to a woman wild with chaotic emotions and actions. But this was a wise woman, so he paid attention. Let's pick it up again right there:

> She continued, "Long ago they used to say, 'Get your answer at Abel,' and that settled it. We are the peaceful and faithful in Israel. You are trying to destroy a city that is a mother in Israel. Why do you want to swallow up the LORD's inheritance?"
>
> "Far be it from me!" Joab replied, "Far be it from me to swallow up or destroy! That is not the case. A man named Sheba son of Bikri, from the hill country of Ephraim, has lifted up his hand against the king, against David. Hand over this one man, and I'll withdraw from the city."
>
> The woman said to Joab, "His head will be thrown to you from the wall."
>
> Then the woman went to all the people with her wise advice, and they cut off the head of Sheba son of Bikri and

threw it to Joab. So he sounded the trumpet, and his men dispersed from the city, each returning to his home. And Joab went back to the king in Jerusalem. (vv. 18–22)

Don't get lost in the beheading of Sheba. That seems like a shocking ending to a story about a wise woman, I know. But keeping in mind the severity of Sheba's crime, it was what the circumstances demanded. The same fate befell Goliath and Absalom and even the previous king, Saul. Their severe choices ushered in severe consequences.

Instead of getting snagged in that part of the story, let's focus on another sentence: "Then the woman went to all the people with her wise advice," and they listened and acted in accordance with her wisdom (v. 22).

This woman had established a pattern of making wise choices in her life, and a pattern of wise choices in the ordinary paves the road to a demonstration of wisdom in the extraordinary. She saved her city's wall and possibly many lives as well. Her wisdom preceded her. When it mattered most—in this time of crisis—she didn't have to try to convince people her advice was wise. They knew it. They trusted her. They trusted her knowledge. They trusted her insight. They trusted her discernment.

She had that deep knowing inside her because she was one wise woman. She didn't have to make it all so complicated. And neither do we. We just have to be discerning.

As we've already discussed, discerning what's best *is* something we're capable of doing. But we must layer into our lives knowledge and depth of insight that form a trustworthy inner discernment. One more time:

Knowledge is wisdom that comes from acquiring truth.

Insight is wisdom that comes from living out the truth we acquire.

Discernment is wisdom that comes from the Holy Spirit's reminders of that knowledge and insight.

OPEN THE BOX

Let's go back to my foyer. Had I relied more on my wisdom-based discernment, I would have seen the irrationality in my fears, opened the box, not made it all so complicated, and not wasted my emotional energy.

That box sitting in my foyer is such a picture of a decision sitting in front of me. Left unchecked, my fears, foolishness, and feelings will cause me to complicate the decision. My wisdom-based discernment will help me process and make the decision.

Don't read past that last paragraph too quickly. Fear, foolishness, and feelings left unchecked sometimes play a big role in our decision-making hesitations. People fear what they don't understand. People let foolishness take them places they don't want to go. And feelings left unchecked will sometimes flat out lie to you.

Therefore we need to flip the fear, foolishness, and feelings in our decision making into a much healthier fear that leads to wisdom. But don't just take my word for it, look at Scripture:

The fear of the LORD is the beginning of wisdom; all who follow his precepts have good understanding. (Ps. 111:10)

Skilled living gets its start in the Fear-of-God, insight into life from knowing a Holy God. (Prov. 9:10 MSG)

Fearing God has been a term I've wrestled with and longed to better understand. I know it means to have a deep level of reverence for God. But I love what a friend of mine who studies language root words to better understand biblical terms recently shared with me. After much study, she now defines a person who fears God as "one who sees the hand of God in everything." There are several Hebrew words for the word *fear*, but let's look at two of these closely. One is *pachad*, which means terror. That's not the one used in this passage about the fear of the Lord. The word used is *yirah*, which means being in awe of God. That deep sense of reverence where we truly desire to look for the hand of God in everything.

Yes, yes, yes. Whether we are facing everyday opportunities or epic obstacles, might we simply do just that. Look for God in it all.

Apply wisdom. Knowledge. Insight. Discernment.

Put our hearts and our minds in places where wisdom gathers. And then with courage, make the decision. Open the box. Move forward. And determine not to make it all so complicated.

Chapter 5

God's Word, Ways, and Wonder

I WASN'T IN THE MOOD TO TAKE ON THE STRESS OF MAK-ing another decision. Seriously, how do these decisions that need to be made keep finding me? Sometimes I wonder if I inadvertently sent out some sort of e-mail invite that read, "Need something? Yes, please ask me. Just reply to this e-mail, text me, call me, Facebook me, tweet me, or hunt me down at church. I would delight in any of the above."

Maybe I should have negated all these requests by put-ting a sticky note on my forehead: "I realize you feel that God put on your heart to ask something of me," it should have said. "I've used my decision quota for the day. Try again later. Or don't. That would be just fine too."

But I hadn't put up my sign. And another question came, a question requiring an answer. A decision. *Ugh.*

Pulling from the great wisdom of Scarlett O'Hara, I thought, *I can't think about that right now. If I do, I'll go crazy. I'll think about that tomorrow. Yes, tomorrow. Tomorrow feels better than today.* So I delayed and put off the decision.

Then I got a text message reminding me a decision needed to be made. I ignored it. I got mad at my husband when he saw the text message and reminded me I needed to make this decision. I pouted and then realized tomorrow the decision wouldn't be easier to make. It would be the same hard decision with a bitter bit of delay sprinkled on top.

A friend of our family's in her early twenties was looking to move out of her apartment and into a less expensive living situation. We adore this young lady. She's spent a lot of time with our family. She's lovely and no trouble at all.

But instead of that deep-down knowing we talked about in the last chapter, this time I felt conflicted. The discernment wasn't clear. I knew I was going to need to take myself through a process of evaluating this decision. And my evaluation would have to be a consideration of my resources. Did I have the resources to handle this request along with my current responsibilities? Could this fit physically, financially, spiritually, emotionally?

Could this fit physically, financially, spiritually, emotionally?

I dug through my purse to retrieve a receipt that had been floating about. I chastised myself for not being more organized and having a piece of paper handy. I mean, seriously. I scrawled out a list of things to be considered when making this decision. Did saying yes to this make sense in each of these areas?

Physically? We had a spare bedroom.
Financially? Her small rent payment would cover any additional expenses.
Spiritually? We are Christians and we want to love other people. This seemed to fall right in line with our core values.

But there was one more aspect to be considered. Could I handle this emotionally? Did I really have the white space to handle one more person living under my roof? After all, it's not just about adding a person. You add that person's stuff, their opinions, their need to use the laundry room, their need for hot water in the morning, and their occasional issues with your daughters borrowing their clothes. Etcetera. Etcetera. Etcetera.

On the surface these things felt trivial. Surely I could get over them. Overlook them for the greater good of doing this nice thing for a person I do care about.

Christians are expected to do nice things.
I am a Christian.
Therefore I should say yes.

But then why was I so stressed out about saying yes? Please

know sometimes God absolutely gives us spiritual resources to say yes that override our limited resources. But not always.

It's not wrong to use wisdom, knowledge, and an understanding of your resource capacity to assess your decisions. Proverbs 24:3–4 (NKJV) reminds us, "Through wisdom a house is built, and by understanding it is established; by knowledge the rooms are filled with all precious and pleasant riches."

And Luke 14:28–30 (NKJV) says, "For which of you, intending to build a tower, does not sit down first and count the cost, whether he has enough to finish it—lest, after he has laid the foundation, and is not able to finish, all who see it begin to mock him, saying, 'This man began to build and was not able to finish'?"

As I continued to count the cost and assess my available resources, I felt I should say no. But I also felt I was expected to say yes. Do I go with what I'm expected to do? Or what I feel I should do?

Whenever there is a conflict between what we feel we're expected to do and what we feel we should do, it's time to step back from the decision. And seek clarity from the only source free of the entanglements of misguided opinions and unrealistic expectations.

God.

Maybe it feels a tad silly to bother God with a decision of this sort. But it's not. It's right in line with what God calls us to do over and over and over.

He whispers, "This, this, this is what it means to have a relationship with Me. That you talk to Me. That you come to Me. Remember, all who are weary and burdened, I will give them rest. I will take the burden of your questions, decisions, and fretting and bring rest from all the confusion. I may give you an immediate answer. Or, I may point you on a path of discovery. Just stay with Me. My Word. My ways. My wonder. And you will know" (Matt. 11:28, author's paraphrase).

God's Word addresses the approach I take with my activities: "Come to me, all you who are weary and burdened, and I will give you rest" (v. 28).

God's ways address the attitude I have with my activities: "Take my yoke upon you and learn from me, for I am gentle and humble in heart, and you will find rest for your souls" (v. 29).

God's wonder is the assurance that not every activity is my activity: "For my yoke is easy and my burden is light" (v. 30).

His Word. His ways. His wonder. His path of discovery. Yes, I need to go there.

GOD'S WORD ADDRESSES MY APPROACH

The Word of God instructs us on what *activities* are in line with His will for His people. And certainly practicing hospitality and opening my home are activities that fit.

But the Word of God also instructs the *approach* we should have to life. How we approach something matters. If the activity we're considering is in line with God's Word but our approach to that activity isn't, we will overdraw ourselves and bankrupt this part of our lives. A good approach to something requires enough resources to handle the demands of that activity.

Using the categories I was considering while making this decision, I needed to determine whether I had the required resources physically, financially, spiritually, and emotionally to let my friend live with us.

> *Physically*: I had a spare bedroom. So, yes, I had this resource. Therefore my approach to this opportunity was realistic and probably wouldn't have led to bankrupting my family's space.
>
> *Financially*: As I said before, her small rent payment would have covered the expenses of having her live with us. Yes, I had the necessary resources. Therefore my approach in this area was realistic and wouldn't have led us down an irresponsible path with our finances.
>
> *Spiritually*: Having her live with us wouldn't drag us down spiritually. It wouldn't prevent us from staying involved at church, reading our Bibles, or having access to the spiritual resources necessary to continue growing in our relationships with God. Therefore my approach in this area was a healthy one.
>
> *Emotionally*: This is where my resources started thinning out a bit. Remember, a good approach to something requires enough resources to handle the demands of that activity.

Being a wife and mom to five kids, aged teen to young adult, requiring my attention; a leadership position at Proverbs 31 Ministries requiring my attention; a serving role at my church requiring my attention; and a book deadline requiring my attention left few emotional resources available during this particular season.

And if I spend resources I don't have, I will eventually bankrupt myself. I don't know about you, but for me I know the danger of getting emotionally bankrupt. It is straight-up ugly. While the activity of having my friend live with us might be honoring to God, my emotional approach eventually would not be.

God's Word stepped in and reminded me of something I must consider: "And whatever you do, whether in word or deed, do it all in the name of the Lord Jesus, giving thanks to God the Father through him" (Col. 3:17).

Whatever I do.

In word or deed.

My approach must honor Jesus.

Yes, God's Word addresses both my activities and my approach. But here's what's interesting. God's Word doesn't always go into detail when addressing our activities. The Bible doesn't say specifically, "If you're in a season of life with a husband who owns his own business, five children, a growing ministry, commitments to your church, and a book that is due that you're way behind on writing . . . and a young, precious girl in her twenties asks you if she can move in with your family for a year, here's what you should do."

I wish the Bible would be that specific with my activities sometimes. But while the Bible might not address my activities in specifics, it certainly does address my *approach* to those activities in specifics.

Whatever I do.

In word or deed.

My approach must honor Jesus.

And honestly, I have a hard time doing that with very little emotional breathing room. Having an extended houseguest would have required attention. It would have required that I have some emotional space to accommodate the added emotional demands of another person under my roof. And if someone or something demands attention that I don't have the emotional space to handle, my actions start betraying my intentions. I will start slipping at reflecting Jesus in my words and deeds.

When we slip at living out the Word of God, we slip at living in the will of God. And there was my answer.

No.

Having an extended houseguest in this season didn't fit. This opportunity didn't fit the emotional space I needed to do this activity with the right approach. At the bottom of the receipt I wrote, "Emotionally—This is where this answer becomes a no." This doesn't make me a bad person. It makes me the wrong person for that assignment.

THE WAYS OF GOD ADDRESS MY ATTITUDE

Now, here's where my mind starts spinning and my heart sinking. I'd decided this was a no answer. I was certain this was a no answer. But then I was not so certain this was a no answer.

Is it loving to say no?

It feels more loving to say yes.

And shouldn't I consider what's most loving since God commands us to love Him and love others? Can't love help me rise above a bankrupted emotional approach?

This is where the *ways* of God must step in and guide us.

We're told, "God is love" (1 John 4:8). Therefore, the ways of God define love. As a matter of fact, *The Message* labels Paul's famous love passage in 1 Corinthians 13 "The Way of Love":

> If I speak with human eloquence and angelic ecstasy but don't love, I'm nothing but the creaking of a rusty gate.
>
> If I speak God's Word with power, revealing all his mysteries and making everything plain as day, and if I have faith that says to a mountain, "Jump," and it jumps, but I don't love, I'm nothing.
>
> If I give everything I own to the poor and even go to the stake to be burned as a martyr, but I don't love, I've gotten nowhere. So, no matter what I say, what I believe, and what I do, I'm bankrupt without love. (vv. 1–3)

I'm bankrupt without love. Focus on that word *bankrupt.* Yes, the activity of letting someone live with me could be loving. It could be in keeping with God's ways. But doing this activity without an attitude of love would not reflect God's love. While a God-honoring *approach* requires the proper resources, a God-honoring *attitude* requires me to reflect God's love.

My attitude of love must be fiercely guarded when considering adding activities. My attitude of love must not be sacrificed on the altar of activity.

Here's where we must get brutally honest with ourselves. Taken the wrong way, this could be used as an excuse to become more selfish. But that's not what I'm saying at all. In other seasons, we've opened our doors wide to missionaries, orphans, widows, and teenagers. But this time we couldn't.

I had to ask myself, *Am I saying no to this because I'm being selfish? Or am I saying no to this because as the one who keeps a finger on the pulse of my family, I know this wouldn't be healthy for us right now?*

When I talk about "attitude of love," it's not an excuse to get out of serving others. It's an exercise of asking God to help me realistically assess how to love a person without bankrupting my family. I am to love this person. We'll see in just a bit that I didn't just totally walk away from this young girl. But I did have to admit, in order to keep an attitude of love, I couldn't have her living with us. My *attitude* of love must trump my *activity* every time.

Look at all the activities listed in the "Way of Love" Bible verses:

* Speaking with eloquence
* Speaking God's Word
* Having faith that commands mountains
* Giving everything I own to the poor
* Becoming a martyr

Those are amazing activities. They are godly. They seem like Best Yes activities. (Well, all except the burning martyr one—*yikes!*) But look at how the Scriptures challenge us to put the attitude of love before every one of these good activities. Because without love, we are nothing and bankrupt.

The ways of God insist on an attitude of love. Therefore, my ways should reflect an attitude of love. Not a ragged, rushed, and rash attitude due to overactivity. Is it loving to say no? *Absolutely,* if doing so protects and preserves a loving attitude for the part of this assignment that is mine.

In keeping with the themes of 1 Corinthians 13, I can challenge myself: *I can take in a houseguest, but if I don't have love, I will do nothing, accomplish nothing, be nothing but a grumpy landlord with a used-up attitude.*

Yes, an attitude of love is God's way. And there's another thing we must know: whatever attitude we bring into a situation will be multiplied. Think about how Jonah brought an attitude of disobedience and almost caused a whole ship full of people to sink. The little boy listening to Jesus on a mountainside generously brought loaves and fishes, and they were multiplied enough to feed thousands. Whatever attitude we bring will be multiplied.

Whatever attitude we bring into a situation will be multiplied.

In my home, if I bring a grumpy attitude, it doesn't take long for everyone else to start acting a little grumpy.

In my office, if I bring a tense approach to a meeting, it doesn't take long for everyone else to start feeling tense.

In a friendship, if I bring a defensive and edgy response, it doesn't take long for my friend to get defensive and on edge.

And if I have a houseguest who pushes my emotional boundaries into stressed-out places, that stress will be multiplied throughout my home. And honestly, it will be multiplied in my houseguest's life as well. And that's not fair, not loving, and not God's way.

God's way is love. My way must be a way of love. As I made this choice, I needed to consider what this choice would cost me in my attitude. My attitude of love must trump my activity. Again, my no was confirmed.

THE WONDER OF GOD, MY ASSURANCE

The Word of God addresses my *approach*. The ways of God address my *attitude*. Now the wonder of God provides my *assurance*. And here's where things get exciting even when it feels hard to say no. God's wonder takes a *no* and turns it into a *know*.

Saying no to my friend can become a way for her to know and experience God's provision. You see, I knew my no would leave an empty space in my friend's life. She'd still need a place to live. She'd still need something to come through.

But we have to know God is especially fond of filling empty spaces. God is a master at providing just the right thing in just the right timing. Sometimes we are that answer and God will provide through us. Sometimes our "yes" answers are the way others will know and experience God's provision.

Here's the core issue—we aren't the master provider. He is.

But here's the core issue—we aren't the master provider. He is. That's why I had to honestly assess all the things we've talked about in this chapter. And whether my answer to future things is yes or no, my assurance is that He is the master provider. For those walking with the Lord, the Bible promises:

> [T]hey are the ones who will dwell on the heights, whose refuge will be the mountain fortress. Their bread will be supplied, and water will not fail them. Your eyes will see the king in his beauty and view a land that stretches afar. (Isa. 33:16–17)

In this case, God's main desire for my friend wasn't for me to provide a place for her to live, but rather for her to experience Him in the process of discovering His provision.

Oswald Chambers wrote about letting what we feel is our duty be put in direct competition with Jesus' commands. If we refuse to leave an opportunity undone so He can be the one who gets it done, we should heed this warning:

> When you obeyed and left all the consequences to God, the Lord went into your city to teach, but as long as you were disobedient, you blocked His way. Watch where you begin to debate with Him and put what you call your duty into competition with His commands. If you say, "I know that He told me to go, but my duty is here," it simply means that you do not believe that Jesus means what He says. . . . Are we playing the part of an amateur providence, trying to play God's role in the lives of others? Are we so noisy in our instruction of other people that God cannot get near them?[1]

Had I said yes, I would have left no room for God's plan to unfold. And His plan was such a sweet surprise for my friend.

I finally got up the gumption to explain to my friend why I had to say no. But that very same day she got a call from an owner of a delightful little condo offering it to her for a rock-bottom price! She was thrilled! This condo was closer to her work and gave her the privacy and space she needed. His was a better provision than my provision.

Oh, the wonder of God brings forth things we couldn't think of, didn't know to ask for, and would hardly believe could be possible. His wonder is my assurance. It doesn't all depend on me.

Not every assignment is my assignment. Notice that doesn't say no assignment is my assignment. I have assignments to generously give and lavishly love and open my home.

I now had the capacity to consider another way to bless my friend. I couldn't have her living with us full-time, but that didn't mean I couldn't offer her something. So, I thought about what I could offer.

I knew part of the reason she'd asked if she could live with us was because she enjoyed being with us. She enjoyed being around a family since she lived so far from her own. And she enjoyed having my husband and me as godly voices of advice for her life.

So, we issued her a standing invitation to join us every Sunday for church and family day and every Monday night for family dinner and discussion. She's also joined us on almost every family vacation we've taken this past year and been with us for many holiday celebrations. It has been a blast! This Best Yes fits so beautifully for us all.

Let me caution you quickly before we end this chapter. Let's not write *no* in permanent marker across our foreheads, set up automatic replies to our e-mails that simply read, "NO!" and start crossing out all our calendar appointments. Discovering our Best Yes isn't about saying no to anything that feels uncomfortable. Or stretching. Or even beyond our abilities to resource.

This book isn't an excuse not to step out in faith. Please, please understand there is a time and a place to say yes. After all, we're reminded that faith without works is dead. There is a time and a place to say yes. We'll get to that in future chapters.

It's about learning to say yes to those things that are truly meant to be our assignments. Not because we're guilted into saying yes. Or pressured into saying yes. Or because we couldn't figure out how to say no, so by default we said yes.

Rather, we sense God's invitation. To say yes. Yes. Yes.

A Best Yes.

But a Best Yes will require having the courage to say no to other things. No to wrong things. No to some seemingly good things. That's the only way to ensure there's space to run and take that leap of faith toward the best things.

Chapter 6

Chase Down That Decision

I'VE NEVER BEEN ASKED TO SPEAK AT A HIGH SCHOOL graduation. But if I were, I think this would be the essence of my speech: Those decisions you are about to make? Chase them down.

I remember it was a sticky, hot day. All the girls wore white dresses underneath the green silky gowns. The guys were supposed to wear their Sunday best with a tie. But, of course, there were those who wore athletic shorts, no shirts, and painted messages on their bare chests. As they walked across to receive their diplomas, they ripped open their gowns and flashed the crowd their chest billboards: "Class of '87 rules." I bet their mamas were proud.

There were claps and cheers and the throwing of the caps. I'm sure the speeches given that day were delightful.

I can't remember exactly, but there were probably the usual sentiments like: you are embarking on a terrific journey, the future is bright, grab life by the horns, and live the adventure. Then the slideshow of pictures flashed before us to the tune of "Friends Are Friends Forever."

The air was electric with possibility. So many young people. So many dreams. So many decisions on the brink of being made—decisions that would point each of these lives in certain directions. That's what decisions do, after all. Today's choices become tomorrow's circumstances. Proverbs 27:12 says, "The prudent see danger and take refuge, but the simple keep going and pay the penalty."

> *Today's choices become tomorrow's circumstances.*

Here's what I wish we could have seen that day: a video diary of where we'd all be by the time our twentieth high school reunion rolled around.

Obviously that wouldn't have been possible. But can you imagine how powerfully effective it would have been to have the keynote speaker say to us:

> The decisions you make today matter. Every decision points your life in the direction you are about to travel. No decision is an isolated choice. It's a chain of events. If you choose wisely, your future will reflect that. But if you

don't choose wisely, the decisions you make now will take you to places you don't want to be later. [Roll tape.]

Obviously, there would be fabulous success stories that would make the crowd roar with inspired applause. There would be Stephanie who waited to marry until she met a man with deep spiritual roots, a tender approach, and a solid character. The decision to wait for this man proved crucial in helping Stephanie survive the cancer she'd battle in her late twenties. Now she was a survivor with a strong marriage and a solid calling to help others facing life-altering circumstances.

And there would be Tony who made the commitment early in his twenties never to live above his means. He never became wealthy. But he was well-off because he wasn't a slave to the massive debt so many of his buddies struggled through. His motto was that finances are like an elephant. You can either stay on top of them or they will stay on top of you. He made decisions in keeping with biblical principles and it served him well. Again the crowd would admire his wisdom, clap and cheer for a job well done.

But then there would be Amanda who had just signed the divorce papers for her second marriage. She'd fallen in love with Brad during college. He was a party guy, so fun to be with. She'd always wanted a man who would go to church with her, but she figured this partying lifestyle was a phase Brad would get over if they got married. Ten years and two kids later that hadn't quite been the case. After he cheated on her, they divorced.

While still reeling from that devastating rejection, she met Tom at work. They slept together on their third date and

Amanda became pregnant. Trusting that the strong feelings they had meant he was her true soul mate, they'd married quickly. She didn't know Tom as well as she should have, but when it feels this right, it just has to be right, right?

Maybe not.

Three years later Amanda met Craig at the gym. She was sick of Tom's irresponsible behavior. He was a horrible money manager. Craig was a financial planner. Tom had gained twenty-five pounds and refused to step foot into the gym. Craig worked out with her three times a week. Tom never wanted to talk anymore. Craig would stay after their workouts and talk about stuff that interested Amanda for as long as she could stay. Decision after decision, Amanda followed her feelings. The crowd just sat silent as the scene closed with her signing her second set of divorce papers.

And there would be Davis. He never thought it was a big deal to cheat in high school. Or college. Or at his job. Sometimes you just have to grab what you want, he reasoned. And that he did. Only last year he'd grabbed a little too much. He would now be facing prison time for embezzling funds to help him keep up his shiny lifestyle. Again, the crowd watching the video would find this part sobering at best, tragic at worst.

A video highlighting the places our choices would take us would make for a graduation speech no one would soon forget.

But I didn't have that revelatory moment at my graduation. I just had a heart full of naïve hope that a girl with great dreams and good intentions would get where she wanted to go. I went with my heart. If it felt good and looked good, it must be good. And had I continued living with that philosophy, I can't imagine how different my life would have turned out.

SHOW ME A DECISION AND I'LL
SHOW YOU A DIRECTION

One of the best things that happened in my early twenties was the guy I thought I was going to marry broke my heart. That devastation at first sent me to bed wallowing in a fit of despair and depression. And then it sent me looking for new possibilities to ease the ache of his absence in the bars my coworkers would frequent after work.

One weekend I hit such a low, I refused to get out of bed. After several days of hiding in that dark apartment bedroom, my roommate came in and announced I needed two things. She yanked the blinds open and said the first was a little light. And then she held up a newspaper ad for a large church in my town. Her second suggestion was clear. In her quirky, Southern drawl, she quipped, "Now this is where you need to be meeting people. Not at them bars you've been going to."

I love that girl for teaching me something profound that day. I needed light. Both in the physical sense and in the spiritual sense. But even more than that I needed a new direction. A direction that would take me where I really wanted to go. Since I didn't understand that quite yet, I only listened half-heartedly and tucked the newspaper ad between my bed and nightstand.

The next day I gathered myself up just enough to drag into work. After work several of the guys were heading to the bar down the street. I needed some fun, I reasoned, so off I went.

A couple of hours later we were playing pool and drinking. One of the guys offered to make me a late dinner back at his place. I honestly wanted to go. I was lonely. I was miserable.

I was hungry. But I pictured my roommate holding up that ad for church and something wrestled my heart into declining his offer.

Had I gone on that date with the guy from the bar, it would have set my vulnerable heart on a vulnerable path. I don't want to presume I know where it would have taken me. But I do know it wouldn't have taken me closer to the truth I needed.

That next night after work, I pulled the ad out and scanned it. The next Sunday I went to that church.

Now, I'm not saying the act of going to church fixes everything. Just as simply looking at a restaurant menu won't give you nourishment. We've got to engage with what's offered if it's going to do us any good. But putting my heart in a place to receive truth certainly got me going in a completely different direction. This was a good place with good directions and solid friends I still have to this day.

I didn't know how to chase down a decision at that point. But had I known, I would have seen the bar scene would lead me to one place, and the church scene to the place I really needed to go.

Our decisions aren't just isolated choices. Our decisions point our lives in the directions we're about to head. Show me a decision and I'll show you a direction. And this isn't just a message for high schoolers who have their whole lives ahead of them. It's for each one of us with any part of our lives ahead of us. We've got to get good at chasing down our decisions. See where they will take us. And make sure that's really where we want to go.

The other day one of my friends asked me if I wanted to try

Our decisions aren't just isolated choices. Our decisions point our lives in the directions we're about to head. Show me a decision and I'll show you a direction.

her caramel-crunch-latte-love-something-fancy-with-whip-on-the-top. Yes, please. I would very much like to try that. But I didn't. Why? Because I know myself very well. I won't crave something I never try. But if I try a sugary delish, I will crave said sugary delish. I will not want just a sip. I will want a whole one to myself. And then I will want a whole one to myself several times a week. So, let me chase down this decision.

I found out that drink has 560 calories. If I get in the habit of having three of those per week for the next year and change nothing about my current eating and exercising habits, I will take in an additional 87,360 calories. Thirty-five hundred calories equals one pound of fat. So, give or take how my body chemistry may process all this, according to math alone, I am set to gain about twenty-five pounds during this next year. When I chase down that decision, I refuse sips of drinks like these.

People laugh sometimes when I tell them this little process of mine and say, "Well, you're just a disciplined person." Not really. Did you catch that part about how a sip for me would lead to enjoying this treat three times a week? I'm not really disciplined. I'm just determined—determined not to go places I don't want to go simply because I didn't take time to honestly evaluate. I've felt the heavy weight of regret and I don't want to return there.

I recognize some things happen to us that are beyond our control. But there's a whole lot that happens simply because we don't know how powerful it is to chase down a decision. There is a chart that will help you do this on page 254.

Think about a current situation in your life. Seemingly isolated choices have culminated in a certain reality. For example, if I woke up in debt today, it's because of a string of choices I made. There would surely be circumstances beyond my control that added to the debt. But chances are I also played some part with the choices I made. I followed a path that led to my current financial reality.

If I wrote out my choices in a step-by-step diagram that another person followed, he or she would probably end up in debt too. Each choice seemed like a decision, but in reality it was a step toward debt.

In his book *The Principle of the Path*, Andy Stanley says this:

> The direction you are currently traveling—relationally, financially, spiritually, and the list goes on and on—will determine where you end up in each of those respective arenas. This is true regardless of your goals, your dreams, your wishes, or your wants. The principle of the path trumps all those things.
>
> Your current direction will determine your destination. And like every principle, you can leverage this one to your advantage or ignore it to your disadvantage. Just as there are paths that have led us *to* places we never intended to be, there are paths that lead us *away* from those places as well.[1]

That's why I'm so thrilled to be on this Best Yes journey with you. There is hope to take new paths that lead to new places. Your decisions will determine direction. Your direction will determine destination. Let's not ignore this reality any longer. It's crucial we make better decisions, because our decisions will set the courses of our lives.

HOW COULD THIS PLAY OUT TODAY?

I don't know what decisions are before you today. But I hope the statement "chase down that decision" will interrupt you and help truth intersect with your thought processes.

Let me show you how this worked with me last week. I was spittin' mad at my man. We had scheduled to watch a movie together, but then he got a phone call, a call he had to take. And instead of being patient and remembering how he had been understanding all the times I'd gotten phone calls I had to take, I just got mad.

I felt put off.

Ignored.

Less important.

This was supposed to be our time together, and I was really looking forward to it. I wanted to know he was looking forward to our time too. That's one of the most important parts of a date for me—knowing that he is looking forward to it. But the longer the call lasted, the more I convinced myself he was just doing this movie date with me out of obligation rather than out of a desire to really be with me.

When it went from "just a minute" to more than forty minutes, I shut down and went to bed. Mad. Really mad. (All the while that verse about not letting the sun go down on your anger was ringing, ringing, ringing in my ears. *Ugh.*)

The next day, Art asked if we could try again. I was still mad. I didn't want to try again. I wanted to stew and be quiet. I wanted my quiet to punish him. To show him just how hurt I really was. I wanted him to feel the weight of rejection that I'd felt the night before.

Sometimes quiet means just letting things cool off until we can calmly talk. That wasn't the case with my quiet.

I was being incredibly selfish. Selfish feels good in a heated moment of hurt, anger, and disappointment. And it made me want to strangle down and silence verses like, "Let the wife see that she respects her husband" (Eph. 5:33b ESV), and "Follow the pattern of the sound words that you have heard from me, in the faith and love that are in Christ Jesus" (2 Tim. 1:13 ESV).

But the verses were there. Truth has a powerful way of interrupting our runaway feelings if only we'll get it in front of us. So I let those verses march in front of me, boss me, re-direct me. And soon I was chasing down this decision to be silent.

Being selfishly quiet today could start a pattern of behavior that I could return to over and over when hard things happen between Art and me. Habits of selfish quietness could lead to shutting down the communication in my marriage. Shutting down the communication in my marriage wouldn't just frustrate—it could potentially fracture our relationship.

When I chased down where my decision to be selfishly quiet might lead, I knew it was a place I didn't want to go. Why take even the tiniest first steps in that direction?

The scariest place in a relationship isn't when the talking is hard—it's when the talking stops. That's why I had to push past mad and make the choice to talk this through.

Remember the verse from earlier, Proverbs 27:12? "The prudent see danger and take refuge, but the simple keep going and pay the penalty." *Prudent* isn't a word I use often, but it means wisdom or a wise person. Andy Stanley says this:

The implication here is that a prudent man or woman understands that all of life is *connected*. He is aware of the cause-and-effect relationship between what he chooses today and what he experiences tomorrow . . . Consequently, prudent people look as far down the road as possible when making decisions. Every decision. After all, they understand that today and tomorrow are *connected*. As the author of Proverbs states, they stay on the lookout for signs of trouble up ahead . . . They ask what I refer to as *the best question ever*: "In light of my past experience, and my future hopes and dreams, what's the wise thing to do?" The prudent draw upon the wealth of data that life has already provided them and then take appropriate action when they see danger ahead.[2]

I like that question, "In light of my past experience, and my future hopes and dreams, what's the wise thing to do?" We will certainly spend time in future chapters seeking to understand what wisdom is, where it comes from, and how we can get it. We will also see in a future chapter how making a decision is like jumping into a river. Before we jump we must assess where that river will take us before we get swept away.

But for now, let's start with this chase. What's a decision you are in the midst of making? Chase it down. If you do this, where will it most likely lead? And then what? And then? Keep going until you walk it all the way out.

This isn't meant to make you afraid to make the decision. We'll talk more about that in the next chapter. But for now, chasing down a decision is meant to do the exact opposite of fearing a decision. It's to help you more clearly discern the package deal that comes with the decisions we make. And clarity should dispel the fear. I'd much prefer to know what I'm getting into than have it barreling toward me unaware.

Even better, if I have the chance to redirect, I'll avoid going places I never intended.

Yes, if I ever have the chance to speak at a high school graduation, this would certainly be my message. But I'll also use it in the coffee shop with a friend, and with my kids, and with my ministry coworkers, and certainly I'll keep preaching it to the one who needs it most of all—me.

Chapter 7

Analysis Paralysis

THE MONKEY BARS. THE PLACE ON THE PLAYGROUND I found most thrilling and most terrifying all at once. I remember watching the other kids laughing as they mindlessly romped up the ladder rungs to get to the first bar. Without a care, they let their bodies swing across from one bar to the next. It looked so effortless, and they seemed fearless and natural.

One after another the kids glided across and ran around for another turn and then another. I pretended to be in my own little world on the swing. But I wasn't interested in the swing at all. I used it only as a perch to stare and try to figure out how they could so easily master this playground thrill.

I wanted to join them. I wanted to play on the monkey bars more than any other piece of equipment on the whole playground.

But I was afraid.

I'd tried it once but it hadn't worked out so well. I'd held up the line. Like the aggravation caused in any traffic jam, the tension was alive. The longer the other monkey-bar climbers had to wait for me just hanging on the first bar, the more I could hear sighs. Cheeks full of air were being blown out behind me.

One boy got so tired of waiting he got his friend to hoist him up to the second bar and off he went. Others thought that was a great solution, so they followed suit. Suddenly not only was I afraid, I was embarrassed too.

All I had to do was release one hand from the first bar and thrust it forward to grab the next bar right in front of me. But I couldn't make my muscles move. No matter how hard I tried to will my hand to move, my thoughts paralyzed me. All I could think of were the bad things that could happen the minute my hand let go. So, there I stayed—for almost an entire recess.

A teacher finally saw what was happening and walked over to me. She placed her hands on my waist and helped me down. I know she thought she was helping me. But it felt like she was just agreeing with what I feared most: "You can't do this."

Falling would have been better. I could have gotten up from a physical fall. But being told that failure must be avoided at all costs kept me from ever getting back up on those monkey bars again. I would sit day after day staring from the swing across the playground. Watching other people do what I wanted to do.

Maybe you have been there. A decision needs to be made. You ponder and pray. You research and get other people's opinions. You analyze the hows and what-ifs. You desperately want to know which is the one right decision to make. The perfect move. The will of God.

And suddenly you find yourself hanging on that first bar,

paralyzed from moving forward. Fear strangles the momentum that propelled you to grab the bar in the first place. There you stay, until someone hoists you down. And they lower you in more ways than one.

THE FIVE PARTS TO MAKING A DECISION

Not being able to make a decision is a feverish symptom but not the real sickness. Fear of failure is the real cause of our analysis paralysis. There have been fascinating research reports released warning parents of the potential harmful messages we send to kids when they never learn how to cope with failure. Consider Chris, a young woman who is terrified to make a decision—any decision:

> Her insecurity and fear of regret are intense and constant, whether she is choosing between brands of pasta at the grocery store or deciding to accept her boyfriend's proposal of marriage. Sometimes Chris thinks she senses a call to missions or full-time ministry, but other times she's not so sure. Recently she told my friend she would rather work her minimum-wage job and live with her college roommate for years than make the "wrong" decision about the next phase of her life.
>
> Chris is an extreme example, but many twentysomethings experience self-doubt severe enough to keep them in personal, professional, relational, and spiritual paralysis. Think about it. For their entire lives, young adults with helicopter parents have been shielded from failure and

regret. To their mind, negative consequences are truly unthinkable—maybe not even survivable! Why else would their parents protect them so completely?

Some church-raised young adults experience similar self-doubt when it comes to making spiritual judgments. Instead of equipping them to make thoughtful, prayerful decisions and then to trust God for the outcome, the church has instilled a debilitating fear of sin or "stepping out of God's will." How can we expect the next generation to move forward with confidence into God's future when they are scared of making a misstep?[1]

I'll admit I read that with my head tilted and whispered, "Huh" at that last part. I do think we should fear stepping out of God's will. But if you desire to please God with the decision you make and afterward it proves to be a mistake, it's an error not an end.

If you desire to please God with the decision you make and afterward it proves to be a mistake, it's an error not an end.

It took me quite awhile to get this. I remember being a young girl wondering how in the world I'd make sure to make all the right choices in life. What if I picked the wrong college? And then picked the wrong town to move to after college? And then picked the wrong job that put me in the wrong circle of friends? And then I'd never meet the husband I was supposed to marry. And then I'd never have the kids I was supposed to have. And then and then and . . . a thousand more mistakes that all spun off picking the wrong college. I would analyze every option until, like Chris, I suddenly didn't want to make any decision for fear of making the wrong one.

I have a friend who told me she had this same analysis paralysis until one day a wise mentor said something that gave her such freedom. He said so many people stress over knowing God's will and what the right choice to make is. But sometimes God gives us two or more choices that would all please Him and be in His will. We get to choose.

My friend said understanding that has given her more confidence to make decisions, especially since she wants to do the right thing all the time. And, in fact, it's strengthened her relationship with God as she exercises stepping out in faith, trusting God to give her the discernment she needs to choose wisely.

The fear of making a wrong decision shouldn't strip the faith right out of our faith. The only way our faith will ever strengthen is for us to use it. We need to apply thought and prayer to our decisions and then trust God for the outcome. We need to set our sights on growing in faith, not shrinking back for fear of failure.

Here are some of my favorite Bible verses, Proverbs 3:5–6, in three different versions:

Trust GOD from the bottom of your heart; don't try to figure out everything on your own. Listen for GOD's voice in everything you do, everywhere you go; he's the one who will keep you on track. (MSG)

Trust in the LORD with all your heart, and do not rely on your own understanding; think about Him in all your ways, and He will guide you on the right paths. (HCSB)

Trust in the LORD with all your heart and lean not on your own understanding; in all your ways submit to him, and he will make your paths straight. (NIV)

These verses hinge on one crucial thing. I don't want us to miss this. Without this one crucial thing we could mistakenly think there are only three parts to making a decision:

1. Analyzing the decision.
2. Making the decision.
3. Owning the decision.

In actuality, I think there are five parts to making a decision. And the first and the fifth are almost the same. They are like the top and bottom buns of a hamburger. They don't look exactly alike, but they come from the same dough. And they hold the process together. They both involve *trust in God*.

1. *Trusting in God* by placing my desire under His authority.
2. Analyzing the decision.

3. Making the decision.
4. Owning the decision.
5. *Trusting God* to work good even from the not-so-good parts.

Look at the three versions of Proverbs 3:5–6. No matter what version you read, it is clear the opposite of trusting God is leaning on our own understanding—trying to figure out things all on our own. And the evidence of whether or not I'm trusting Him is shown by where I place my focus. After all, we steer where we stare.

WE STEER WHERE WE STARE

Boy, do I know how off course we can get when we stare at the wrong thing. Last week I was driving with two friends to do a webcast at a church in California. There would be hundreds of women joining us live in the audience and more than twelve thousand joining us online. We could not be late. And just to be absolutely certain we wouldn't get lost, we were following the rest of our team in a big red Suburban.

We stayed right with them. If they sped up, we sped up. If they got in another lane, we got in that same lane. Only once did we get separated by a semitruck, but even then we quickly caught up and got right behind them once again. They took an exit, so we took that same exit. They drove through neighborhoods, so we drove through neighborhoods. At one point it almost seemed as if they were trying to play some sort of game and purposely lose us. But we were not easily deterred. We stayed right with them.

But things got a little confusing when they pulled in to the driveway of a house instead of the church. And then things got really strange when the people who got out of the car were not our ministry team.

They glared at us as if to say, "I don't know who you freaky people are or why you are following us, but one step closer and we'll have you arrested."

Well, isn't that just ten shades of awesome?

We put the car in reverse, waved while mouthing how sorry we were, and drove until they were no longer in sight. Then we called the friends we thought we were following and explained we might be a bit delayed. Why? We lost sight of the right red SUV for just a few minutes behind a semitruck. And look how offtrack we got when we stared at the wrong red vehicle. We steered where we stared.

If I'm trusting myself, I will stare at all the possible ways I could fail. If I'm trusting God, I will stare at all the possible ways He'll use this whether I fail or succeed.

When I stare at failure, I'll fear it. I'll convince myself it's the worst thing that could happen. And I'll stay stuck. But when I stare at all the possible ways God can use this whether I succeed or fail, I'll face my decision. I'll convince myself that it's better to step out and find out than to stay stuck. And I'll reach for that next bar.

All those years ago on the playground, it would have been better if that teacher had just said, "Lysa, staying stuck in your fear is way worse than any other choice you could make right now. If you let go of that bar and happen to catch the next one, you'll move forward and prove to yourself that you can do this. Or, if you let go of that bar and fall, you'll see that the ground isn't so far away. It won't feel great to fall, but it won't be worse than all the stress and exhaustion you're experiencing just hanging there on the first bar."

Years later my youngest daughter was playing on the same kind of monkey bars with a friend. I wasn't there to see exactly what happened, but her friend's mom called to say Brooke had fallen. Later, when I took her to the doctor, he confirmed what the swelling in her arm had already told us. It was broken. But here's the amazing thing: Brooke's arm healed and today she still climbs the monkey bars.

I still won't attempt them.

Sometimes it's easier to overcome a fall and a break than the fear of failure. How many times have we found ourselves in the exact same place with decision making? We get both hands on the first bar and, determined to pursue something, we swing out. But then suddenly we find we can't move.

I stare at the ground. I think it all depends on me. I don't feel capable. I feel uncertain. Fear grips the fibers of my muscles and strangles them into paralyzed strings.

I want to shift from trusting myself to trusting God, but how? Fear makes the gap between where I am and trusting God seem an impossible chasm.

THERE IS NO SUCH THING AS A PERFECT DECISION

Recently I surveyed people through Twitter and Facebook with this question: What do you think is the biggest reason people struggle to make decisions? Overwhelmingly, as in almost every answer, was *fear.*

Fear of the unknown
Fear of failure
Fear of getting hurt
Fear of what others will think
Fear of rejection
Fear of missing out on something better
Fear of making the wrong decision

I absolutely understand all these fears. I wrestle with them myself. And some wrestling with fear is good. It can keep us from temporary bouts of stupidity. For example, my kids' fear of being restricted often keeps them from missing curfews. That kind of wrestling with fear is good. But then other times I can still feel like that little girl hanging on the monkey bars wrestling with fear to the point I'm paralyzed from moving forward.

Here's the thing that keeps me from staying stuck: there is no such thing as a perfect decision. As crazy as it sounds, I've stayed stuck in analysis paralysis so many times trying to figure out which choice is the perfect one. And if I couldn't pick the perfect one, I'd rather stay stuck. Or at least that's what my irrational mind thought. But in actuality, being stuck on bar one was the most disappointing place to stay. Perfection is an illusion.

Are there good choices and bad choices? Yes, of course. We talked about that quite a bit in the last chapter on chasing down our decisions. But at this point in my life, I'm not getting tripped up as much in the good versus the bad decisions.

More often now, I find myself stuck between a good choice and another good choice, trying to figure out which one is perfect.

* Should we stay home for spring break and have a relaxing week or go on a simple vacation full of memories? Good and good.
* Should I let my girls take dance lessons they would love but that would require us to eat on the run or tell them no so we can have family dinners at home? Good and good.
* Should I teach that Bible study every Tuesday night at church or be at home to help my kids with their homework? Good and good.
* Should my twenty-year-old daughter go on a date with the guy from our church or just keep things between them on a friendship level? Good and good.
* Should I sleep one more hour so my mind will be sharp today or get up to do that early-morning boot camp so my body will be in shape? Good and good.

What about bigger good and good things?

* Should I go on a mission trip or to a marriage conference? Good and good.
* Should I quit my job to start that ministry I keep talking about or bring more of a ministry heart into my existing job? Good and good.

These good and good decisions happen every day. But here's a secret answer you must know when trying to pick the perfect choice: *there is no perfect choice.* And if you understand this, it will set you free from the fear of making a mistake.

As long as you desire to please God with your decisions, no decision you make will be completely awful. Nor will any decision you make be completely awesome. Every decision is a package deal of both. Every thrill has an element of risk. Every leap of faith has moments of uncertainty. And every great success story has elements of failure. In other words, since there is no perfect choice, I don't have to be paralyzed by the fear that I'm not making the exact right decision.

Again, I want to please God with this decision. But I also want to demonstrate my trust in Him by actually making a decision—having made peace with the fact it won't all be perfect.

There is no perfect job.
There is no perfect school.
There is no perfect spouse.
There is no perfect ministry.
There is no perfect church.
There is no perfect way to raise kids.
There is no perfect house.
There is no perfect route.
There is no perfect decision.

Each of these choices will have just enough imperfections to make them some combination of good and not so good. Even if you are following God and He clearly directs you to make a certain decision, that choice will not be perfect.

There is no perfect decision—only the perfectly surrendered decision to press through our fears and know that God is working in us to bring about good through us.

Let's state it one more time: *there are no perfect decisions.* And I think it's so important to understand this for two reasons.

The first reason is that it may help us not be so deathly afraid of making a mistake. Even right choices will have elements of things that might feel difficult. And second, it may free us up a bit from second-guessing our decisions when the imperfections of those choices present themselves.

If you were to ask me about my marriage, I would say I'm so thankful I married Art. He is godly. He is a man of strong character. He still makes my heart melt sometimes. But there are also times I am hyperaware of his imperfections.

And he's aware of mine. He's crazy about me. He thinks I'm fun, adventurous, and funny. I add romance to his life. And he still thinks I'm lovely in form and feature. (I think that's the biblical way of saying sexy.) Yes, he's crazy about me. But sometimes he's crazy *because of me*. I have a long list of really quirky things about me that require him to demonstrate great patience.

I only like bananas with green stems and absolutely no brown spots. I can't stand mint of any kind. And I can't help but remind whomever I'm riding with that I much prefer the person driving go the speed limit. Never to be exceeded by more than 4 miles per hour. Please and thank you. And that kind of amazingness can require a certain level of patience. Which he has for my quirks and I have for his.

While we made a good decision in marrying each other, it wasn't a decision that always feels perfect.

BUT WHAT ABOUT MISTAKES?

On the flip side, I can also make decisions that don't feel perfect because they are mistakes. For example, after much pleading and begging I agreed to let my girls get a hamster even though we have three dogs. Things went well for a while. But one day they didn't. And after my daughter decided to share our family crisis as a prayer request at school, I got a note from the teacher informing me I was no longer qualified to be a weekend watcher for the class guinea pig. Bad decision to get a hamster and suffer the shame of the teacher ban, right? Maybe.

But there was a good part to even this bad decision. It was better to get a letter and not be able to take the class creature home than to have taken the guinea pig and have it pass to the sweet by-and-by because of our dogs. And all God's mamas say, "Amen!"

Here's the bottom line. Good decisions will often have elements of not so good. And not-so-good decisions have elements of good. Either way, if I'm hoping to be able to know the perfect choice and then move forward with certainty, I'll probably not move forward.

Here's where the certainty is: My imperfections will never override God's promises. God's promises are not dependent on my ability to always choose well, but rather on His ability to use well.

God will use the good and not-so-good parts of the decisions we make. A very popular verse reminds us of this. Romans 8:28 says, "And we know that in all things God works for the good of those who love him, who have been called according to his purpose."

Don't miss this crucial part—"for the good of those who love him." We must have at the core of our hearts a love for God and a surrender to God if we want to be guided by God.

Also don't miss the context from which this verse is

My imperfections will never override God's promises. God's promises are not dependent on my ability to always choose well, but rather on His ability to use well.

pulled. Verse 28 starts with the word *and*, which tells me that it's tied to the verses that precede it. Verses 26–27 remind us that when we are feeling uncertain or weak, the Holy Spirit will lift up prayers for us in accordance to God's will. Let's read the whole paragraph as it goes together.

> In the same way, the Spirit helps us in our weakness. We do not know what we ought to pray for, but the Spirit himself intercedes for us through wordless groans. And he who searches our hearts knows the mind of the Spirit, because the Spirit intercedes for God's people in accordance with the will of God. And we know that in all things God works for the good of those who love him, who have been called according to his purpose. (vv. 26–28)

If your heart and your mind are aligned in the direction of God, you don't have to agonize to the point of paralysis over the decisions before you. We will steer where we stare. So stare mightily at God and His plan. And if you don't know His plan, stare mightily at living out His Word in your life and His plan will unfold day by day. Decision by decision.

Take one of your hands, release your grip, and reach. That next bar will be there. And should you fall, the ground isn't so far away.

Chapter 8

Consider the Trade

A FEW YEARS AGO I TRAVELED TO VISIT A FRIEND IN Connecticut. As soon as she picked me up from the airport and we started driving, I saw the fallout from the storm she'd tried to describe—a massive twenty-inch snow in the middle of fall. But it wasn't the amount of snow still on the ground, or the snowmen still proudly standing, or the huge snowbanks on either side of the road that grabbed my attention.

It was the broken trees. The branches were piled everywhere. House after house. All down the street. Disastrous piles of limbs—big piles of trees—all still clinging to the leaves that hadn't dropped yet. And because the leaves hadn't dropped, the trees broke.

That's what happens when a snow comes early. The trees weren't designed to face snow before releasing their leaves. They weren't made to carry more than they should. And neither are we.

I know the weight of carrying more than I should. And usually it's because I've refused to release something before taking on something else. If I want to choose a Best Yes, it's crucial I make room for it first. Otherwise, a Best Yes can quickly become a stressed yes. And a stressed yes is like snow on a tree that refuses to release its leaves. It causes cracks and breaks at our core.

I remember watching this TV show a couple of years ago in which an expert lady was instructing a messy lady about how to get organized. At the core of what was being taught were the habits of highly organized people. I was fascinated. But not fascinated as in taking notes and making plans to implement what was being taught. No, I was fascinated like the girl who eats ice cream while watching an infomercial about the latest and greatest exercise video curriculum. I admired the promised results but didn't really think I could make the kind of sacrifices required.

So, I just watched.

The organized lady taught her little lessons and then decided to help the messy lady implement what they'd just discussed. The next scene was the messy lady revealing, for all the world to see, her closet. I was about to have a slight heart attack on behalf of my new messy TV friend. I don't show even my best friend my closet, and based on the way they set this segment up, I felt sure messy lady shouldn't be showing hers.

I was yelling at her through the TV, "Don't do it! Don't go in there!" But just like the people in scary movies who open the door to the basement and start walking toward the dark unknown despite the audience's pleas to turn back, messy girl didn't listen to me either. There she went—straight to her crazy space called a closet, opening it up for all the world to see.

I could tell from the expression on the expert lady's face, she was pleased with such a dramatic situation. Drama makes for good TV because crazy people like me stay tuned in. I'm like white on rice when I see crazy. And this closet was crazy. Kind of like mine.

The expert lady swirled and twirled about like a fairy godmother, commanding the wrong items be taken out and the right items be placed in color-coded order. I sat there fascinated by how her expert mind could so clearly see potential in this tangled space and know all that needed to be done to turn it into a dream closet.

The final scene was the big reveal to the messy lady. She oohed and aahed over the progress made. And though she resisted the expert lady during the process of getting rid of many things, the final outcome was worth it. The release phase was hard. But the peace that came afterward was so worth it she stopped lamenting over those things she'd given away.

Then the expert lady made the ex-messy lady hold her hand up and pledge one final thing before the show ended. She repeated these words to the expert: "I promise before adding anything new, I will make space by getting rid of something first."

A silly show about organizing became yet another lesson for me on the necessity of release. If we refuse to release before we add, we will get overloaded. The ex-messy lady can't expect to keep that beautifully redone closet beautiful if she starts adding more and more to it. I can't expect to have room for my Best Yes opportunities if I refuse to release the clutter.

WE HAVE A CHOICE

Here's what's hard. Here's where the ex-messy lady struggled. And here's the reason I sat on my couch observing other people getting organized rather than walking into my closet and actually implementing what I was learning.

How do we discern what to call clutter and what to keep? And in a bigger sense, how do I know how to discern a Best Yes?

Obviously this applies to much more than just my closet. In the last chapter I told you about my struggles to choose between good and good. Now, I want to cover that tension of feeling like I'll regret missing out on an opportunity if I release it to make room for another. I don't always want to let that opportunity or that thing go. I wrongly think I can just add more and more and not get overloaded.

That fear of release keeps me in a place of clutter and chaos. In regard to my closet, my thought process runs something like this:

That orange shirt is great. I like it a lot.

But I haven't worn it in over a year.

But is that because it was hidden among lots of other stuff? Or because I just don't feel drawn to wear an orange shirt most days?

If I get rid of it and then need it, I'll just kick myself. I don't want to have to eventually buy another one when this one is perfectly good. So, maybe I should keep it just in case.

But then maybe I should keep everything just in case.

After all, it wouldn't be in my closet if I didn't think it was great when I bought it. Oh, organizing my closet is just too hard.

I trade having a peaceful space for the slim possibility I'll give the orange shirt away and regret it. Yikes! That's not a good trade. Ever.

We aren't in the habit of release. Why? Because of the fear of missing out on some things. But in the process we miss out on the best things. If we want to discern our Best Yes assignments, we must consider the trade.

We see how refusing to release gets people in trouble all throughout the stories in Scripture. Eve refused to release the forbidden fruit. And because she became hyperfocused on that one thing, she wound up missing out on the best things in paradise. Terrible trade.

Esau refused to release his urgent need for some stew. And because he became so hyperfocused on eating that soup immediately, he wound up missing out on his birthright. Terrible trade.

Moses refused to release his fear that just speaking to the rock as God commanded wouldn't actually bring forth water. And because he struck the rock twice, he wound up missing out on entering the promised land. Terrible trade.

David refused to release his inappropriate desire for Bathsheba. And because he set off a chain of sinful events including adultery and the murder of Bathsheba's husband, he wound up suffering the horrific experience of losing a child. Terrible trade.

Each of these people paid a high price for their refusals to release—to let go of their ways so they could walk in the amazing way of God. They took on the heavy and often harsh weight of not trusting God because they didn't consider the trade. Unfortunately, they couldn't see their trades as clearly as we can. But maybe studying their mistakes and hard consequences will help us notice the consequences of our own trades when we refuse to release.

Please, please hear me on this. These stories have outcomes that can feel too harsh for a loving God to allow. But understand, it wasn't God's desire for any of these people to suffer the consequences they did. Each of us has a free will, which means we have the freedom to make choices.

God tells us the right way to go, but we have to make the choice to do so. Choices and consequences come in package deals. When we make a choice, we ignite the consequences that can come along with it.

Choices and consequences come in package deals. When we make a choice, we ignite the consequences that can come along with it.

The good news is we have a choice.

The bad news is we have a choice.

It's a double-edged sword. It was true for Eve, Esau, Moses, and David. And it's true for you and me. Refusing to release often means refusing to have peace. I trade my peace for a weight of regret. And it's a bad trade. But I still do it.

MAKING PEACE WITH RELEASE

Sometimes I flat out say no to releasing something though I'm very aware of the consequences that choice will bring. I know, for instance, I need more sleep. But I don't want to stop watching that TV show that keeps me up too late. I ignore the little prompts in my brain telling me to go to bed. Then I feel tired the next day. I'm grumpy. I'm short-tempered with the kids. I refused to release; therefore I have less peace.

Other times I resist releasing something by putting the decision off. I delay, delay, delay. I don't want a messy closet. But I don't want to have to decide what items to purge. So, I do nothing.

But not making a decision is actually a decision. It's the decision to stay the same. And staying the same when I know I need to change is a choice that carries consequences with it. Not the least of which is a gnawing regret that will grow bigger and bigger with each passing day.

Not making a decision is actually a decision. It's the decision to stay the same.

Now catch this: Purging my closet will cause me to give away some things, including that orange shirt. Giving away the orange shirt may cause me regret. But that regret will diminish over time. In no time at all, I won't be thinking about the orange shirt. On the other hand, if I keep a closet that is so chaotic I'm embarrassed for even my best friend to see it, this regret will just grow bigger and bigger as my closet gets messier and messier.

It's the same principle for someone who wants to get healthy and decides to give up sugar for a season. Walking away from a triple-layer chocolate cheesecake may make you regret not trying it in those first few minutes after you pass on dessert. But that regret will diminish when you leave the restaurant and go home with a stomach that's not bloated from overindulging.

Now let's turn that around. If I indulge in that cake tonight . . . and then six cookies tomorrow . . . and, well, since I've blown it, I might as well have some ice cream too . . . You can see that this string of choices will cause a regret that grows with each sugary indulgence.

In other words, the only way to diminish our regrets is by making decisions that lead to peace. And peace requires from us some sort of release.

Release isn't stealing from us. It's a gift—a gift to a woman weighed down, grasping her leaves in the midst of a snowstorm, desperate, so desperate for help. She can feel the twinges and hear the creaking sounds of a splitting break about to happen. She knows she can't take much more. Tears well up in her upturned, pleading eyes. "God help me. It's all too much. I'm tired and frustrated and so very worn-out."

The wind whips past her, trailing a whispered, "*R-e-l-e-a-s-e.*"

She must listen or she will break. Her tree needs to be stripped and prepared for winter. But she can't embrace winter until she lets go of fall. Like a tree, a woman can't carry the weight of two seasons simultaneously. In the violent struggle of trying, she'll miss every bit of joy each season promises to bring.

No, release isn't stealing a thing from her. From me. Or from you. Release brings with it the gift of peace. The beautiful, bare winter branch can now receive its snow. When we release in peace, we signal we're now ready to receive. Receive what's next. Receive what's best. Receive what's meant for this season, right now.

I don't know what you have to release right now. But I suspect you know. Just like I do in a few areas of my life.

I walk to my closet and pull out the orange shirt. I walk straight to a box labeled "give away." And with the fling of my wrist, I release it. With release comes more peace. I see that now. I believe that now.

And I refuse to lament the orange shirt. To someone else, it will be a needed blessing. To me, it was a space stealer. This one shirt is but the beginning. I start my habit of release. Trading this orange shirt for peace is a very good trade indeed.

Chapter 9

Show Up to Practice

IN THE LAST CHAPTER WE STARTED ANSWERING THE question, how do I discern a Best Yes?

Great question, but this question doesn't have just one answer. It has layers of answers. The first layer we discussed was "consider the trade." If I say yes to this, I will have to release that. Will that trade be worth it? It is worth releasing clothes I don't wear very often so that I can have a more orderly closet. Though it may not be easy to purge, the trade is worth it.

The next layer is "show up to practice."

Remember when I mentioned that my daughter Ashley is a pole-vaulter? Well, that means she has learned how to sprint down the track in spiked shoes, plant the very long pole she's carrying into a small pit, bend the pole down enough to create a force to lift her body off the ground, twist so her head is down and her feet are now pointed toward the sky, arch over a bar at least eight feet off the mat, and throw the pole away from her at the last minute while she crashes down onto the mat, hopefully back-first and not face-first.

Whew.

And did I mention she has to do all that without jostling or hitting the bar she's careening over, lest the bar fall and her jump not count? It's no joke.

The first time I watched her, I literally held my breath until my face turned bright red. And I might have slightly tee-teed in my pants. Three drops. But enough to realize this sport was going to take some getting used to.

Her first year of pole vaulting was hard. She held last place on the team the whole year. Though she tried and tried and tried, she could barely clear eight feet—a height the other girls were getting with ease. At one meet she literally landed on top of the crossbar, straddling it much to the simultaneous amazement and disbelief of the spectators. The crossbar usually falls if you so much as tap it. But somehow it stayed in place even after she lifted one leg over and fell to the mat below. The jump counted, but it was still too low of a height to move up in ranking.

Her second year was also hard. Again, she held last place on the team almost the entire year. Though she started clearing eight feet on some days, she still couldn't clear the bar at higher levels on a consistent basis. As a result, her teammates all qualified to go to the year-end state meet. But she did not.

She's now into her third year. And some things are finally clicking. She's moved up to being consistently ranked second on her team. But last week something else happened. Something amazing.

The meet started out a little shaky for all the girls as we were visiting another school with equipment much older than ours. Plus the mat exploded with collected pollen every time someone landed on it. Not the best conditions.

It took Ashley a couple of tries to hit eight feet, then eight feet six inches. She moved on to nine feet, which on her third try she cleared. At nine feet six inches, I could tell she was nervous. Really nervous. This was her personal best so far. I think in her mind, this was as high as she could see herself going.

She missed the first attempt.

On the second attempt, she cleared the bar but twisted too much in the air. Her pole crashed against the bar while her body landed half off the side of the mat. Her cleats cut her calf and she came around the side limping. But somehow the bar hadn't fallen. The jump counted. She cleared nine feet six inches and was called to line up for a ten-foot attempt. No girl on her team had cleared ten feet at a meet. And Ashley had never even gotten it at practice.

She limped to the starting place and went through her normal routine of lifting her pole up in the air and putting it down. She rubbed her sore leg. She marched in place and slid her sweaty palms down her shorts.

As her mama, I could feel the tension, the nerves, the pressure. When she finally broke into the sprint down the track, nothing looked any different from any other time she'd run. When she planted her pole, nothing looked any different from any other time she'd planted her pole. But when she cleared ten feet with ease, the expression on her face was so very different from any expression I'd ever seen.

She popped off the mat and erupted in a jubilant scream

I'll probably never forget. She ran from behind the mat straight into the arms of a mama who may or may not have been making a slight spectacle of herself. Screams of joy. Tears of amazement. Three drops of, well, you know.

It was mind-blowing. She took first in the meet and set a new school record. This girl, who for years struggled in this sport, was now the new school-record holder.

As her mama I'm proud of her accomplishment. I am. But you know what makes me most proud? It's not that she broke the school record. It's not that she took first place. It's not even that she cleared ten feet, a height I wasn't sure she'd ever get.

Those things are amazing. But they aren't what make me most proud of her. What stirs my heart the most is the fact she just kept showing up at practice and giving it her all.

She just kept showing up. Running down that track, planting her pole, twisting her body, trying to clear the bar, crashing onto the mat, and receiving feedback from her coach. And then putting her coach's instruction into practice. Run after run. Attempt after attempt. Day after day. Sometimes succeeding, sometimes failing, sometimes feeling great, sometimes in pain, most times in last place—but no matter what, she was committed to showing up to practice.

And then in a moment when it mattered most, she knew what to do. She knew what to do that day at the meet because she'd been training her mind and her body day after day in practice.

If we want to know what to do when it matters most, we've got to be committed to showing up to practice. A Best Yes is a wise yes. The Bible reminds us, "Get all the advice and instruction you can, so you will be wise the rest of your life"

(Prov. 19:20 NLT). And wisdom needs to be practiced day after day if we are going to know how to apply it to the Best Yes decisions when they come.

———————

Wisdom needs to be practiced day after day if we are going to know how to apply it to the Best Yes decisions when they come.

———————

THE WOMAN OF WISDOM

In Proverbs chapter 9, we see two distinct opportunities. We are all students trying to pursue a journey of wisdom. The choices we make will determine if we end up with the virtue of wisdom or the vice of folly.

The teacher in Proverbs personifies the virtue of wisdom and vice of folly as women. Much like we personify liberty as Lady Liberty, here the writer is personifying wisdom and folly. We need to identify with these passages as students of the patterns being described. The woman of wisdom is described in verses 1–6:

> Wisdom has built her house; she has hewn out its seven pillars. She has prepared her meat and mixed her wine;

she has also set her table. She has sent out her servants, and she calls from the highest point of the city, "Let all who are simple come in here!" she says to those who lack judgment. "Come, eat my food and drink the wine I have mixed. Leave your simple ways and you will live; walk in the way of understanding."

Now let's look at the woman of folly described in verses 13–18:

The woman Folly is loud; she is undisciplined and without knowledge. She sits at the door of her house, on a seat at the highest point of the city, calling out to those who pass by, who go straight on their way. "Let all who are simple come in here!" she says to those who lack judgment. "Stolen water is sweet; food eaten in secret is delicious!" But little do they know that the dead are there, that her guests are in the depths of the grave.

Isn't it interesting that though these women are vastly different, they have some similarities?

They are in the same location—the highest point in the city.
They both have the same goal—to get people to come into their houses to eat and drink with them.
They both say the same thing at first—"Let all who are simple come in here!"

But what they have to offer is vastly different. Wisdom has put in the preparation time. She has done the work and she has something legitimate to show for it. Folly has not. She was lazy. She has not done the work, therefore she either has nothing to offer or can only offer stolen goods.

As I look at the descriptions of each of these women, I'm struck by the words that characterize their lives. The woman of wisdom builds and hews out pillars, which tells me she cares about and pays attention to the details. She is prepared and organized and gets others to help her. Her ways lead to life and understanding. But the woman of folly is loud, undisciplined, and lacks knowledge. She sits around and doesn't make progress. Therefore, she doesn't have much to offer because she isn't prepared. Her offerings are stolen. Her ways lead to death.

Imagine for a minute if I decided what I experienced at Ashley's track meet was so exciting that I, too, would like to be a pole-vaulter.

Ashley and I show up at the next meet together out on the track. My daughter would never in a million years allow this to happen. Somewhere between my cellulite legs, my overzealous squeals, and my three-drops thing, she would have made sure security ushered me far away from her teammates, I can assure you. But, for the point of my illustration, let's continue hypothetically.

So there we are, looking slightly similar. Like the woman of wisdom and the woman of folly, we both

* are in the same location—on the track at the high school near the pole-vaulting pit.
* have the same goal—to get our bodies up and over the bar using a pole without killing ourselves or injuring others. And to clear more height than others in the process.

⁊ say the same thing at first—"Let all who are interested
in seeing the pole-vaulters come here!"

Along with all those similarities, I can also call myself a
pole-vaulter. And I might even be able to squeeze myself into
a large size of those little athletic Daisy Dukes they call a
uniform. But what my daughter and I have to offer is vastly different. She, like Wisdom, has put in the preparation time. She
has done the work and she has something legitimate to show
for it. I, like Folly, have not. In the pole-vaulting world, I have
been lazy. I have not done the work, therefore I have nothing
legitimate to offer.

WISDOM REQUIRES WORK

Remember, a Best Yes is a wise yes. Therefore, if we are going
to be able to discern what a Best Yes is, we've got to have
wisdom. And wisdom requires work. If I want to be able to
exercise wisdom, I've got to be practicing it in my everyday
life. I've got to show up to practice.

How do we do that? Well, first the Bible tells us if we lack
wisdom to ask for it (James 1:5). God will give us wisdom just
as He gives us muscles. But just because I have muscles doesn't
mean I can do all that my daughter with muscles can do. She
has trained her muscles to be strong and capable so when she
calls on them, they don't fail her.

Likewise, we've got to train our wisdom muscles to be
strong and capable so when we need them most, we'll know
how to use wisdom. We've already talked about knowledge,

insight, and discernment and how these help us apply wisdom to our decisions.

Proverbs 2:1–11 gives us clear instruction on the way to have wisdom, use wisdom, and be protected by wisdom:

> My son, if you accept my words and store up my commands within you, turning your ear to wisdom and applying your heart to understanding—indeed, if you call out for insight and cry aloud for understanding, and if you look for it as for silver and search for it as for hidden treasure, then you will understand the fear of the LORD and find the knowledge of God. For the LORD gives wisdom; from his mouth come knowledge and understanding. He holds success in store for the upright, he is a shield to those whose walk is blameless, for he guards the course of the just and protects the way of his faithful ones. Then you will understand what is right and just and fair—every good path. For wisdom will enter your heart, and knowledge will be pleasant to your soul. Discretion will protect you, and understanding will guard you.

I can have wisdom. I can use wisdom. I can be protected by wisdom.

You can have wisdom. You can use wisdom. You can be protected by wisdom.

But we've got to show up to practice. As the verses above show us, we can have, use, and be protected by wisdom if we do these things:

✦ Accept God's words. (God's Word is a gift. But it won't

do us any good if we don't accept the gift, open the gift, and use the gift.)

- Store up His commands within us. (We must get into God's Word and let God's Word get into us. The more verses we memorize, the more our thinking will align with His truth.)
- Turn our ears to wisdom. (Listen to wise teaching, wise advice, and keep the company of wise people.)
- Call out for insight. (Ask others to help us see the "trade" we talked about in the last chapter and the consequences we'd be igniting with each choice.)
- Cry aloud for understanding. (Ask the Lord to show us how our choices will affect others.)
- Look for wisdom as passionately as we would hunt for a hidden treasure. (See the value of wisdom as higher than any worldly way we are offered. Stay focused on looking for wisdom despite the many distractions the world puts in front of us to make decisions without taking the time to apply sought-after wisdom.)

After all these qualifiers, the Scriptures say, "Then you will understand the fear of the LORD and find the knowledge of God. For the LORD gives wisdom; from his mouth come knowledge and understanding" (vv. 5–6).

I find it interesting that these Scriptures use the specific wording here, "The Lord gives wisdom." Have you noticed that sometimes *Lord* is in small caps in the Bible and sometimes it isn't? Where our English translations read *Lord*, the Hebrew Scriptures say *Yahweh*. That's God's personal name. The original scribes of what became our Old Testament didn't fully write out God's name when they were copying the text because of the Third Commandment. They figured, if no one ever speaks God's name, then no one will ever take it in vain. If you walk into a synagogue today and hear a Jew reading from the scrolls, that person will say "Adonai" whenever he or she sees *Yahweh* in the text. *Adonai* means "lord." That tradition has been maintained in your Bible for one reason: the name of God is powerful. As Isaiah states, the name of God gives wisdom.

THE ABSOLUTE BEST YES

Do you remember in the story of Adam and Eve when Eve encountered the serpent? Just before that in Genesis chapter 2, God is referred to as "the Lord God." Over and over He is "the Lord God." Eleven times we see "the Lord God." Why? Because God was on a first-name basis with Adam and Eve.

Then Genesis 3 starts with the serpent (aka Satan) entering the scene. Once again we see God referred to as "the Lord God," but then something shifts.

"Now the serpent was more crafty than any of the wild animals the Lord God had made. He said to the woman, 'Did God really say, "You must not eat from any tree in the garden"?'" (Gen. 3:1).

Do you see what Satan just introduced to Eve? Doubt, yes. Questioning God, yes. But there's something else more subtle and, might I dare add, more dangerous. He omitted God's name. In other words, Satan will acknowledge God. But he lacks a personal, intimate relationship with Him and wants to make sure we don't have one either. If we don't know God personally, then we are unlikely to be influenced by Him.

It's Yahweh who gives wisdom, not some untouchable figurehead of a "god." If we aren't walking in wisdom, intimacy, and understanding with our Lord, we are walking in folly. And folly's ways lead to death.

It is difficult to embrace an intimate relationship with someone we never see. God understood this, so He physically came to earth and took on another name: Jesus. The absolute Best Yes we'll ever give is asking Jesus Christ to be "the LORD God" over our lives. When we receive Him, we receive life everlasting. But this is just the starting place. We must walk with Him daily, using His gift of wisdom with each and every decision.

My sweet Ashley is a teenager with typical teenager struggles. I don't want to paint her as overly ideal or perfect in any way. But she really is something to watch on that pole-vaulting track. Her pole-vaulting muscles are now strong. But her wisdom muscles are in the early stages of development.

That's why it's so important to Art and me that at least one of us always shows up at her meets. The mental part of a sport requires more than just body muscle. It requires wisdom as well.

Two days ago I watched her slip back into struggling to just clear eight feet six inches again. She would start running and stop in frustration. Then she'd back up, start running again, and stop in frustration. Over and over she repeated this until tears were streaming down her cheeks.

I watched Art quietly get up and walk to the fence lining the track. He called to her. She locked eyes on him. "You got this, Ash. I've seen you do this before and I'll see you do it again. Just let your body do what it knows to do from all that practice."

She wiped her tears. She walked back to the track. She shook her legs. She looked at us with tears welling up in her eyes again. She lifted her pole. She took off. And she sailed over the bar.

Sweet friend, you got this. You've made a Best Yes decision before. If nothing else, you've picked up this book because your heart wants to make decisions that honor God. Just show up to practice. Practice wisdom with all you've got in you. Wisdom will become the rhythm of your mind just like pole vaulting is the rhythm of Ashley's body. Then you'll know.

You'll know. Just let your mind do what it knows to do from all that practice. And if I'm there with you, I'll be cheering. And hollering. And jumping. And then probably crossing my legs. (And you'll know why.)

Chapter 10

Managing Demands Means Understanding Expectations

THE SPACE BETWEEN OUR EXPECTATIONS AND OUR REALI-
ties is a fertile field, and it's the perfect place to grow a bumper
crop of disappointment.

When I was in high school, I had a friend whose sister had
the coolest hairdo. It was cropped short with straight bangs
that fell messy over one eye. She was that older sister who just
seemed to have a handle on how to do everything with style.

I somehow decided all her coolness traced back to her
hairdo, as if that were the budding spot from which the life I
wanted could sprout. Yes, that hairdo. Never mind the fact her
hair was thin and obedient, and mine was thick and rebellious.
Never mind that her hair was sleek and straight, and mine was

114

curly at best and frizzy at worst. Never mind that her bangs fell nicely over her forehead, and mine had a crazy cowlick causing them to grow up, not down. Yes, never mind reality.

I set my expectations high and willed my hair to fall in line. The hairdresser chopped. And chopped. And chopped. And tried to assure me I now looked *just* like the picture of the older sister. But that was a lie. I knew it. She knew it. And, oh, how the space between my expectation and my new reality grew some serious disappointment. I still have nightmares of that disastrous hairdo where I wake up desperately grabbing at my head to make sure my hair is still there.

But hair grows back. Bad cuts can be fixed in time. That disappointment can be remedied.[1]

Other situations aren't so easy. Maybe you have some space between a current reality and an unfulfilled expectation. If so, I imagine disappointment can be found growing there.

The space between our expectations and our reality is a fertile field, and it's the perfect place to grow a bumper crop of disappointment.

Psalm 23:1 (NKJV) says, "The LORD is my shepherd; I shall not want." The Hebrew word for *want* is *chacer*, meaning "to lack, be without, become empty." So, if the Lord is my shepherd,

I shall not become empty. I shall not live in a constant state of disappointment where circumstances drain me dry.

But I do sometimes. And not just with my hair. It's other stuff as well—important stuff. How do I let the Lord shepherd me so the gap between my expectations and reality closes?

First, I have to assess the expectations and responsibilities that come with each thing I say yes to. This is an important step in determining whether this choice I'm making is a Best Yes. I also need to identify unrealistic expectations so these can either be managed or eliminated before I jump into an opportunity.

These are crucial things to consider when making Best Yes decisions.

EXPECTATIONS

Every yes answer comes with a list of expectations. If I don't know what those expectations are, I can't possibly meet them. It's crucial to identify the expectations before giving a yes answer.

Then I must determine which of those expectations are realistic and which ones are unrealistic. Those that are realistic should be planned for. That means I write down as many of the demands that I can think of for this yes answer and put them on my calendar. If it's a project, then I make a project timeline. If it's a social event, I not only schedule the event but also schedule time to get or make whatever it is I'm supposed to bring. If it's a financial commitment, I make out a budget according to what I can afford and mark down when the payments are due.

Yes, I make a plan for what's realistic so I don't overextend myself.

I wish I had understood this at the tender age of eighteen. I drove to college in an electric blue Firebird that was cool fifteen years before I became the owner. Let's just call it the FB. It had power nothing. I'm not even sure it had air-conditioning. And I won't take time to tell you about the 8-track tape player it had as a little bonus. Because, well, I suspect either (a) you have never heard of such a thing or (b) you would rather forget you are old enough to know what that is.

Just know that this car got me where I needed to go but didn't make me look good getting there.

I see how selfish all that sounds now. Good gracious, couldn't I have been thankful to have a car at all?

I was thankful when I first got it. I had saved to pay for half of the cost. My parents paid the other half, and I was simply thrilled to have a car to call my own. Plus, it was right in line with the kinds of cars my friends in high school drove. They all had their own situations with the wheels barely hanging on. But that was high school.

By the time I drove to college, FB left me wanting. I went to a university where the students didn't drive cars like FB. My best friend my freshman year drove a new sports car. I wasn't dumb enough to think I could ever have a sports car. But couldn't I have something a little better than FB? I mean, at least something with a cassette player?

This desire grew and grew my whole freshman year. During that summer, I went to a dealership with not a dime to my name to see what I could afford once I traded in the FB. Have mercy on my stupid little self. The salesman helped me see that I could afford a lot even if I had next to nothing. I bought his bag of tricks and traded FB for a used, little, white sporty thing with a bad paint job and a big ol' car payment.

The minute I signed the papers and drove off the lot, I owed quite a bit more than what the car was worth. But never mind all that. I had a cassette player and—hold your breath—electric windows. Make that an electric window that only worked on the driver side. Not the passenger side. Which I found out two days later when I rolled it down halfway and it refused to roll back up.

Awesome.

I then had to get a friend of mine to help me shimmy the window back up and duct tape it to the top of the door. Call me classy.

My mom and dad about lost it when I called to tell them my great news. My dad said, "Let me tell you what's going to happen. You are barely going to be able to afford the car payment each month. You will struggle even more to pay for your gas and insurance. You will be working to have a car to drive to work. And then this new little treasure is going to break down. It will! And you aren't going to have the money to pay for the repairs. Then what?"

I thought it an awfully bad time to ask for a loan to pay for my broken-down window. So I swallowed hard and said, "Dad, that's not going to happen. The guy at the dealership said he'd never seen such a good car for such a low price."

I could practically hear the eyes rolling in my dad's head. Have you ever heard that sound? Yes, it just makes you feel all swell inside, huh?

What do you think happened just a few months later when

I was driving home for Thanksgiving? The transmission blew. Completely. As in, the car refused to go one more mile and I was still a good two hours from home. Because that's what cars do to girls who overextend themselves financially. They create opportunities for us to learn lessons. The hard way.

And learn I did. I had to borrow $1,500 from my dad to get the transmission fixed. That debt might as well have been a million dollars. I was working at a truck stop back at college making a whopping $2.00 an hour plus tips. It would take a whole lot of time serving fried eggs, ham biscuits, and cups of coffee to pay back $1,500. All so I could drive a white car with a duct-taped window and a bad paint job.

Because I had not clearly defined what it would mean to take on this used car, I was oblivious to the expectations this would place on me and my budget. And I got myself into a heap of trouble that haunted me for many a waitressing day afterward.

Understanding the expectations for each yes we give is crucial. Here are some great questions to ask when determining if the expectations we're agreeing to with this yes are really realistic or not:

- It feels thrilling to say yes to this now. But how will this yes feel two weeks, two months, and six months from now?
- Do any of the expectations that come from this yes feel forced or frantic?
- Could any part of this yes be tied to people pleasing and allowing that desire to skew my judgment of what's realistic and unrealistic?
- Which wise (older, grounded in God's Word, more

experienced, and more mature) people in my life think this is a good idea?

+ Are there any facts I try to avoid or hide when discussing this with my wise advisors?

I'm sure there are other questions along this line to think through when determining realistic expectations. Tweak this list as it applies to your situation. But please don't skip this process. Yes, it takes time. But it's worth it.

Evaluation eliminates frustration.

Evaluation eliminates frustration.

UNREALISTIC EXPECTATIONS

We should also evaluate unrealistic expectations. Unrealistic expectations become unmet expectations. And unmet expectations are like kindling wood—it only takes but a spark of frustration to set them ablaze and burn those involved.

One of the worst job situations I ever got myself into was an opportunity riddled with expectations that were unrealistic for me. The job required me to be good at accounting, filing, and organization. If only they'd made me show them my personal checkbook, my piles of papers at home that knew not what a filing cabinet was, and my disorganized closet. I might have interviewed well, but I was not the one for this job, and I knew that.

I knew their expectations weren't realistic for me.

I knew, sans a miracle, this whole situation would be extremely stressful.

But, by golly, this job opportunity was there. And it paid well. And I needed a well-paying job. So, I took it.

And it about killed me. No, I'm not being overly dramatic with that statement. I mean my heart pumped at a pressure so high during my daily charades of trying to put on a qualified front for this job, I thought I might have a cardiac episode. It was awful. I knew it. And my employer quickly knew it too.

I resigned before they could fire me, but that whole debacle taught me a valuable lesson for evaluating unrealistic expectations. Not just for potential jobs but in all areas of my life. If there is a lingering list of unrealistic expectations, it must be discussed and negotiated through until the expectations either become realistic or get dropped from the opportunity at hand.

What makes an expectation unrealistic? When an opportunity stretches me to a breaking point, it becomes unrealistic. Usually for me the areas I have to consider are:

* *My time.* The schedule required to meet all the demands of this opportunity isn't in line with the time I have to invest.
* *My ability.* I'm not equipped with the necessary skills to carry out the functions of this opportunity.
* *My money.* I can't afford the financial responsibilities that come along with this opportunity.
* *My passion.* The responsibilities of this opportunity evoke a sense of dread instead of fulfillment in my heart.

→ *My season.* There is something that must take a higher priority during this season of my life, therefore the timing is off for me to take this opportunity.

Looking at these areas helps me see an opportunity from all angles. Identifying potentially unrealistic expectations helps me know what to discuss in advance before saying yes, before there is a gap between what I'm able to deliver and the expectations of others.

HOW DO I APPLY THIS TO A DECISION I'M MAKING TODAY?

My friend Genia has been an avid exercise girl her whole life. She's one of those people who absolutely gets excited about working out. I don't understand this. I work out to keep myself sane and try to manage my weight. I like the benefits, but I can't say I always like exercising.

Genia loves it. And she loves her local YMCA where she takes classes and spends hours sweating. For years as she walked into her YMCA, she admired the pictures of the board members who run the business side of this gym. And she secretly hoped that one day they would ask her to be a board member.

Last week she got the invite she's dreamed of for a long time. They asked her to consider being a board member. She was thrilled as she read the e-mail. Her heart pumped fast as a huge smile spread across her face.

Her first inclination was to shoot back a quick e-mail saying, "Yes, I'm incredibly honored you would ask me!" But she waited so she could take time to assess whether this exciting opportunity was a Best Yes for her in this season of her life.

Part of this assessment was carefully reading the attachment with all the expectations of a board member and the dates for the next two years' worth of meetings she'd be committing to attend.

As she placed that e-mail next to her calendar, her smile dimmed. God kept whispering other things to her heart in that quiet time of consideration. "Give the best of who you are to what you're already committed to."

For a couple of days Genia kept thinking about what she felt the Lord was telling her about giving the best of herself to her prior commitments. She kept looking at all the dates and all the expectations. And here's where she landed.

The expected meetings didn't match the amount of time she had to give. They would quickly have become an unrealistic expectation for her, and the thrill of being asked would quickly wear into a dread of disappointment. Her limited ability to serve would become a disappointment to herself, to them, and to the other commitments to whom she had already promised her time.

So, she graciously declined this opportunity.

As we processed this situation a few days later, she was so thankful she'd clearly understood the expectations beforehand. Indeed, evaluation saved her a lot of frustration.

Let's look one more time at those five questions to ask before making a commitment:

> ✢ It feels thrilling to say yes to this now. But how will this yes feel two weeks, two months, and six months from now?

+ Do any of the expectations that will come from this yes feel forced or frantic?
+ Could any part of this yes be tied to people pleasing and allowing that desire to skew my judgment of what's realistic and unrealistic?
+ Which wise (older, grounded in God's Word, more experienced, and more mature) people in my life think this is a good idea?
+ Are there any facts I try to avoid or hide when discussing this with my wise advisors?

Pick a choice you are in the midst of making right now and honestly assess the expectations through the filter of these questions. Maybe even add to these to make them more specific for your situation. Print them off. Talk through them with a friend, mentor, or parent. And let evaluation eliminate potential frustration.

Now, one more thing as I think back to my high-school-hair situation. Consider this your open invitation to boss me. The next time I start flashing pictures of cute pixie haircuts I'm considering, somebody remind me of this story. Please. Pretty please. With a dollop of hair gel on top.

Chapter 11

The Power of the Small No

IT WASN'T GOING TO BE A FUN CALL TO MAKE. I HAD SOME questions about a bill we'd gotten from someone we'd hired to do work on our home. They'd made a lot of mistakes, and when they attempted to fix them, things still weren't right. We were having someone else right these wrongs, which was costing us money we didn't have. We'd paid to have the work done once. Now we'd have to pay to have the work undone and redone.

To make matters worse, now we'd gotten this unexpected bill from him that we owed a little more than the originally agreed-upon price. My stomach in knots, my head pounding, and my heart racing, I picked up the phone and dialed.

Suddenly it felt as if I had a mouth full of cotton balls. And a heat lamp on my face.

There was nothing in me that wanted to place this phone

call. I watched my finger hit the last number and prayed for voice mail to pick up. One ring. Two rings. *Come on voice mail, voice mail, voice mail.* Three rings.

"Hello?"

Words swirled and emotions began to make my voice crack and sound strangely high-pitched.

"Um, yes. Hi, this is Lysa, and I'm calling about the work you recently did at my house." My heart was drumming so hard I wondered if the call could count as my cardio workout for the day. I'm nothing if not pitiful.

I continued, "Well, you see, there's a, um, problem?"

Instead of stating it like a grown-up, I let my sentence curl into a question.

"There's no problem." The guy quickly interrupted me, clearly not understanding that I wasn't asking him if there was a problem. I was trying to state that there *was* a problem. But before I could clarify, he continued, "I'm glad you called. I've been meaning to call and ask about giving me a letter of recommendation for some prospective clients."

The call was not going well. And he had prospective clients? Now, not only was I struggling to ask about the overages on our final bill, but I'd also have to disappoint him by saying we couldn't endorse his work.

He was a nice guy. And I hated the thought of disappointing him. But endorsing him wouldn't be truthful. After all, what if people hired him only to have the same kind of experience as we did? Then they'd probably be angry with us and could wind up refusing to pay him or, worse yet, sue him. Endorsing him would not be doing him any real favors.

It was time to exercise the power of the small no.

A small no pushes through the resistance of awkwardness

and disappointment because it's better to nip something early on. Early on, expectations and disappointments can be managed better with a small no. But the more we let things develop and progress, the harder the no becomes.

"I'm so sorry. I think you are a really nice person with great intentions. But I have to be honest and let you know we are not satisfied with the work you've done. That's actually why I was calling. And, gosh, I really, really didn't want to have to make this call. Please know we want to honor you by paying what we agreed to pay and maybe coming to a compromise with the overages. We don't want you to be hurt financially by this at all. But I can't be put in the position to be asked for an endorsement. So, as hard as it is, I'm saying no to you now so I don't have to say a damaging no to a potential client asking for an endorsement of you later."

I'm sure my admission was as hard for him to hear as it was for me to say. But he did thank me for being honest with him before I was put in the position of getting into a hard conversation with his potential clients. He admitted he'd probably taken on more than he could realistically accomplish with our job and admitted he knew he hadn't done the job with excellence. We came to an understanding about the bill, and in the end he felt we had been very fair.

This no was hard. But in the grand scheme of how things could have unfolded, it was a small no.

I've learned there is power in the small no if only we'll choose to use it. The power is in saying no before things grow to the place where a no becomes even harder to give, more painful than if given early on, or so much is already put in motion that now the no feels nearly impossible to realistically implement.

As I talk with friends about this concept of the small no, there's an interesting dynamic at play each time a small no should be given. Almost without exception it's when the minute we receive a request, we know deep down our answer should be no. But we delay—as if delay will somehow make this request go away so we don't have to deal with it.

But delay hardly ever makes a request go away. Quite the opposite. It does three things that are unfair to the people waiting for our answer:

- It builds their hopes that our answer will be a yes.
- It prevents them from making other plans.
- It makes an eventual no much harder to receive.

When we know we can't do something, using the tactic of delay, unlike sugar, will not help things go down better.

What small no might you need to exercise in your life right now?

I know it feels like either delaying your no or just saying yes and dealing with the consequences would be better than saying no. Boy, do I ever understand that dilemma. Most of us were raised to be nice. And somehow we've taken up the notion that saying no is not nice. But what if a small no can be given in such a way that it becomes a gift rather than a curse?

SMALL "NO" ANSWERS, GOOD GIFTS

I work with an amazing friend named Glynnis. She's the senior editor of content we publish through Proverbs 31 Ministries.

Part of what makes her such a brilliant editor is being able to spot articles that are a great fit for our readers. She finds it thrilling to contact one of our writers and let them know they will be published.

But there's a not-so-fun part of her job as well. For every article she agrees to publish, there are many more she has to decline. This is no fun. Writers pour their hearts, souls, and best efforts into stringing words and sentences together. They hold their breath as they hit Send and submit their work. And it's so disheartening to do all that and get nothing but several sentences of rejection sent back.

I know that rejection hurts from all the years I tried and tried to get someone interested in my writing. Give me a chance. Just some kind of shot at getting published.

Glynnis knows it personally, too, which is what makes her heart so sensitive and wise when writing rejection letters. She's made a personal commitment to be one of the best in the Christian publishing industry at writing e-mails declining the opportunity to publish someone.

She doesn't just say the typical "Thanks, but no thanks." She invests in them with her small no. Glynnis tells them how they can improve their writing. She gives them a gift alongside the no that has led to people thanking her for the investment she made in them. As I said before, small "no" answers are good so you can manage people's disappointments and expectations. But they can also be investments if spoken so they benefit the one being told no.

We must not confuse the fact that saying no isn't the same as being hurtful. The Bible reminds us that we shouldn't "let any unwholesome talk come out of [our] mouths (or fly from our typing fingertips), but only what is helpful for building others up according to their needs, that it may benefit those who listen." That's from Ephesians 4:29, with my own little addition in parentheses for the sake of our social-media-driven world.

It is possible for a small no to do just that—build others up according to their needs. It is possible for a small no to benefit those who listen.

Glynnis leverages the small no as an opportunity to build and benefit in powerful ways. She makes saying no a wonderfully positive thing. Just like *The Message*'s version of Proverbs 24:26, her "honest answer is like a warm hug."

How? Because she works at her "no" answers to make them good. She finds things to encourage. She points out the potential. She wraps her honesty in gentleness while remaining confidently clear that this is a no. She speaks of her own need for grace. She gives hope. And she covers it all in love and prayer. Back when our ministry had a magazine, this is what one of her letters of decline would have said:

Thank you very much for submitting your article, ("____"), to the *P31 Woman* publication. We are honored to be entrusted with your writing.

. . . When I read your article, there were things I really appreciated, like your obvious love for God's Word and your family. You have a delightful storytelling ability. Plus, I admire your dedication to pursuing God's call to write. However, after careful review, I'm sorry to say this piece isn't a good fit for the unique needs of our publication at this time.

. . . Please know that I see the potential in your

writing, and encourage you to continue to write as much as you can. One thing I would suggest is to stick with one topic within the body of your article, giving it more clarity and focus. This will make your insightful teaching around this topic connect more clearly with your reader.

. . . You are welcome to submit other pieces you have written.

. . . God's blessing to you as you pursue your writing, and thank you again.

Isn't she amazing? Glynnis's example challenges me to stop getting all panicked about giving out "no" answers and to work on making them more positive. I did okay with the contractor from the beginning of this chapter. I wrapped my honesty in gentleness and was confidently clear with my no. But I think I could have found more good things about his work to point out. Made more of an investment.

Now before we get on with implementing the small no, I want to throw out two cautions we must keep in mind: We can't use our "no" answers as wands to wish away our responsibilities. Nor can we use our "no" answers as weapons.

We can't use our "no" answers as wands to wish away our responsibilities. Nor can we use our "no" answers as weapons.

MY NO SHOULDN'T BE A WAND OR A WEAPON

There is a time and place to want to please people. You shouldn't send your boss a text message saying you read a great book today empowering you to say no, so "no to the job!" You've decided to go shopping rather than come to work.

If we are getting a paycheck, we have an obligation to do the work we agreed to do. And if we've given our word to serve in a capacity, we need to honor our word. We must not take this permission to say no and use it as a wand to wish away all our responsibilities.

Churches still need people to serve in children's church. Schools still need moms to volunteer. World relief organizations still need people to sponsor kids. Your kids still need dinner. Your husband still needs . . . you know what. Bible studies still need leaders. Houses still need to be cleaned. Friends still need birthday celebrations.

So let's do what needs to be done with a happy heart, thankful for each of these opportunities and the evidence of life they represent. Whistle while we work. Do a great job. And be nice. Yes, all that and more. Just remember not every responsibility can be your responsibility.

I love what one of my blog readers, Christa, said her husband suggested:

> I am thankful for my husband who helps me say "No." During the busiest time of my life . . . working full time and kids were little, he helped me set limits. I could only say "Yes" to one thing in each area of my life. One position of service at church, one volunteer activity at the kids'

school, one project at home . . . everything else was No.
It helped me really look at the things I wanted to do, set
priorities and only do the things I was truly called to do.[1]

Christa didn't use her no as a wand to dismiss any and all
responsibilities. Rather, her no was a realistic way to set limits
within her areas of responsibility.

I also must remember not to use my no as a weapon.
Learning to say no is a wonderfully freeing ability, but one that
must be used with grace. I have a friend whose sister started
receiving professional counseling, which is a great thing to do.
However, she took a few things her counselor taught her to
an extreme. Once she felt empowered to say no, she suddenly
turned into a *No!* ninja, karate-chopping anyone who even
came close to asking her for something. She used her "no"
answers in demanding, demeaning, and hurtful ways. And all
her relationships suffered as a result.

---

*While my heart wants to say yes, the
reality of my time makes this a no."*

I've learned the best "no" answers are graciously honest.
A simple no I will sometimes use is, "While my heart wants to
say yes, the reality of my time makes this a no." Because I am
someone who carries a great desire to make others happy, my
heart is usually always jumping up and down demanding, "Say
yes! Say yes! Say yes!" But my brain has learned it must boss my

heart around a bit once it checks my schedule, considers my capacity, and understands what is and is not my responsibility.

Another gracious no I like came from my blog reader Connie, who commented:

> A friend shared this with me and there was a time when I literally kept a copy of this by my phone. . . . *I'm sorry but I can't give it the attention it deserves.*[2]

This graciously honors the person's request by acknowledging it deserves attention but allows us to honestly admit we can't be the one to give the necessary time.

We will cover more of this in the next section on implementing the small no, but for now, let's make a promise not to use our "no" answers like wands or weapons.

IMPLEMENTING THE SMALL NO

Okay, so this all sounds good in theory, but how can I practically implement this? I'm so glad you asked. Here are a few scenarios and suggestions:

༄

I have a friend who writes a precious blog. Seriously, she is so endearing and lovely. She also lives in a town that's a popular city for people to drive through on trips. She started getting lots of requests for coffee get-togethers from readers who'd be passing through and would love to have just a few minutes of her time.

That sounds like fun. And her heart is such that she'd

never, ever want to hurt or disappoint her readers. But she's committed to homeschooling her girls. And she noticed every time she did one of these coffee meet-ups, it always lasted longer than she anticipated. Then being short on time when she got home, she'd have to rush through the school lessons, causing her to be grumpy with her girls all afternoon.

So she started giving people delayed answers. Like, "I would love to meet up with you but I don't know my schedule yet for that week. Can you e-mail me back closer to when you're coming and we'll see what we can work out?"

But delaying saying no wasn't going well. It just ate up more of her time going back and forth e-mailing. Then people got their hopes up to the point where she just felt horrible saying no closer to the time of their trip.

When I introduced her to the concept of the "small no," she tried it. When she'd get a request that was unrealistic based on her schedule, she graciously answered with the truth:

> While I would love to get together for coffee, my previous commitments with schooling my girls make this one of those seasons when I must decline lovely invitations. But thank you for thinking of me. Just knowing you'd want to get together is an encouraging gift. Safe travels.

ç๐

A single friend of mine was in a completely different life circumstance. She was having challenges with people always assuming she could say yes since she didn't have a husband and kids at home. But between her job and helping her brother who has a disability, trying to do everything else people were asking of her left her depleted and resentful. She started saying no to everything and everyone. She knew deep down this wasn't what God would want her to do but couldn't figure out any other solution.

When she learned of the power of the small no, she told me it actually helped her see a way for her to start saying yes again. She decided that Fridays from 10:00 a.m. to 3:00 p.m. would be her yes days. She didn't have to work on Fridays and didn't have responsibilities with her brother. Whenever anyone made a request of her, she provided them with what she could offer:

> I would love to help you out. In order to keep better balance in my life, I've started scheduling Fridays as my service opportunity days. Let me know what part of your request can be done during 10:00 a.m. to 3:00 p.m. on a Friday and I'll be happy to get you scheduled. Here are two available Fridays I'd be delighted to use for your request: _____.

I like my friend's approach. While at first it may feel a bit businesslike, consider what researcher Brené Brown found: "The most connected and compassionate people of those I've interviewed [in my research] set and respect boundaries."[3] Interesting, huh? She further argues that the difficult moment of saying no is worth it if it helps you avoid being resentful later.

If you've found yourself saying no to everything in an effort to establish some boundaries, remember Ecclesiastes 7:18: "Whoever fears God will avoid all extremes." We can't only say no to things. There is a time and place to say yes . . . and maybe this small-no principle can help bring balance back to the way you answer requests.

ॐ

I decided I needed a pre-set yes. Being in ministry for a long time, I get requests from people just getting started wanting my advice and help. And I love helping. But if I said yes to everyone who asked, I would literally become an answering service rather than fulfilling my existing assignments.

So once a year my ministry puts on a conference called "She Speaks" where we set aside concentrated time to help teach, mentor, and encourage all those interested in speaking, writing, and leading a ministry. It's my pre-set yes.

This conference is the fruit of the power of the small no in my life. I figured out that the maximum number of potential speakers, writers, and leaders I could help if I attempted personal, one-hour meetings with each would be forty in a year. But with this conference, I can take those same forty hours concentrated around preparing and delivering messages at a conference and reach 650 people. And in the process give those 650 people so much more information and insights during a full two-and-a-half-day conference than they'd ever get in just a one-hour meeting with me.

So, I give small "no" answers while simultaneously offering people a much bigger Best Yes with the conference.

I know all this saying-no stuff can be challenging. I'm sure you're wrestling through a situation right now that doesn't feel as clear-cut as some of what we've been discussing. But press on. Keep processing how the power of the small no might work for you. It will be worth the thinking time, I promise. Because we're on a new path of discovering Best Yes answers for our lives. And the more we practice the power of the small no in the small things of life, the more capable we'll be at exercising the small no when bigger things arise.

SMALL "NO" ANSWERS FOR BIG DECISIONS

The contractor situation from the beginning of this chapter was a small no for a relatively limited situation. But what about using a small no for a big decision?

Art and I have a friend named Wes who has been fascinated with pilots and planes since he was a little boy. For years he dreamed of the life he's now living as a flight-school instructor. Daily he gets to experience the thrill of climbing into the cockpit—the power of defying gravity, the serenity of disappearing into the clouds, and the freedom to travel back and forth from another city in a fraction of the time it would take to drive. Plus, he now also gets to usher others through the process, from dreamers to students to pilots. It's thrilling.

But recently it's all become a bit more complicated. The owner of the flight school decided to offer Wes the opportunity to buy him out. It's an amazing opportunity. But a scary one. Wes is extremely capable. But he's young—in his twenties. Honestly, some people have asked if he's my son, which I'm not sure how to take. Either I look that old, or they assume I had a child in middle school. I only mention this in case you meet Wes someday and are tempted to ask if I'm his mother. I'm *not* mentioning this because it bothers me enough to find a mirror or stretch back the sides of my face and wonder if I need a lift. No, I'm simply saying he's young enough to have thought he'd have many more years before an opportunity like this would come along. Years to gain more experience and save up money.

Art and I both have spent lots of time processing this decision with Wes. Art has helped him with a potential business plan and financial projections. I've helped him with processing different costs to this endeavor: the cost to him personally, the cost to his young wife, and the cost of everyday pressures people who own their own businesses feel.

As we were talking one day, I shared with him a picture I keep in my mind when making decisions. Imagine this opportunity as an amazingly attractive but fast-moving river. There is so much that looks extremely appealing about this river, you're going to be tempted to jump right in. But once you are in the river, you have diminished your ability to make decisions. That river is moving so fast that it will take you where it is going. And if you haven't carefully traced out in advance whether you want to go through and to the places that river flows, you'll be in trouble.

College students declaring their majors should trace the places that career will take them through and to. If you think you want to major in chemistry but hate working in a lab or hospital, trace that river's path before jumping in.

Dating couples who are thinking about marriage should trace out what the term "settle down" means to each of them. If one is thinking mission field in a third-world country and the other a townhouse in middle America, trace that river's path before jumping in.

Moms who are thinking about a new business opportunity should trace out all the expenses of getting started, including upfront costs, child care, and inventory. If a mom's desire is to stay at home with the kids but this business will require her to be gone every night of the week, trace that river's path before jumping in.

Before jumping into the river you have the ability to walk up and down the banks of the river with ease. You have the ability to stick your toes in and consider what this water will be like. You can talk to other wise people who know things about this river. And sit quietly listening for God's voice, reading His Word, and looking for confirmation on what to do.

But once you jump in, the current has a way of demanding your full attention. It's not that you can't make adjustments once you're in the river; it's just a lot harder to go a different direction once you're in.

Several verses that remind us of God's leading, directing, and guiding beside the water have been great comforts to me:

- "He who has compassion on them will guide them and lead them beside *springs of water*" (Isa. 49:10, emphasis added).
- "The LORD is my shepherd; I shall not want. He makes me to lie down in green pastures; He leads me *beside the still waters*. He restores my soul; He leads me in the paths of righteousness for His name's sake" (Ps. 23:1–3 NKJV, emphasis added).
- "With weeping they shall come, and with pleas for mercy I will lead them back, I will make them *walk by brooks of water*, in a straight path in which they shall not stumble, for I am a father to Israel" (Jer. 31:9 ESV, emphasis added).

These are comforting to me because a lot is talked about in the Christian world about stepping out in faith—which I believe in wholeheartedly. People quote the Old Testament story of the priests crossing the Jordan needing to step in, and then the waters parted (Josh. 3:14–16). I love that story. And I believe God clearly instructed them to jump right in. But that doesn't mean God calls *everyone* to jump right in.

Sometimes the greater act of faith is to let God lead us, talk to us, and instruct us *beside* the water. Before we jump in. Before we're in over our heads. Because that's where we can exercise the power of the small no.

With our friend Wes, he's decided not to proceed with buying the flight school right now. He doesn't feel this is a never answer, but it's not his Best Yes right now. He traced the path. He assessed where all this would lead. And he determined saying no now would be much better than saying no later. Especially when saying no later would find him potentially drowning in debt with very few options to get out of that financial pressure. A no at that point would definitely not be small.

So he's not jumping into the river as a new owner. But he is going to stay employed there as a manager and add tremendous value. He's going to give as much as he would if he were the owner. But he's going to do it from the riverbank unless God clearly tells him to jump all the way in.

As I think about Wes's situation and all we've talked about with the power of the small no throughout this chapter, I want to end with the gentle reminder that God does have invitations He wants us to say yes to. I know we've talked a lot about the power of the small no. But we can't forget why we give small "no" answers. It's so we can have the white space and wherewithal to recognize God's assignments and give Best Yes answers to those.

Chapter 12

The Awkward Disappointment of Saying No

MY FANCY SHOES TENTATIVELY STEPPED ONTO THE RED carpet. This was a strange place for my feet that much prefer flip-flops. My consignment-store dress snagged on one of my heels as I took my first step. My face flushed. Not for the first little misstep in front of such a huge crowd but because of the sudden realization of just how disappointed the crowd was. I knew it. They knew it. And it was all so incredibly awkward.

I'd been invited to an awards night for musicians. I was one of just a couple of authors there for one book category. But the main focus on the night was the artistic talent of musicians. My art of stringing words together felt insignificant. Since my words had no beat, they seemed to have no place in the memory of those lining this red carpet. The crowd wasn't there because of the authors. They wanted music. They knew music. They cheered for the musicians.

They were hungry to meet those who sang. Not authors. I got it. I'd be cheering for the musicians, too, if I were in the crowd. And, oh, how I wished I was lost in the comfort of the crowd rather than being the painfully out-of-place girl stepping onto the red carpet.

They had cheered when the vehicle I was riding in pulled up. But as I stepped out, their whoops and hollers quieted. I was a sad disappointment, an unfamiliar face among bright musical stars.

I busied myself fidgeting with my purse and my dress and my cell phone. Awkward does this to us. It makes us fidget. In the midst of trying to comfort what feels so uncomfortable, we just feed the monster. Awkward gorges himself full in those insecure moments.

And then as if things couldn't get any worse, about seven steps down the red carpet, one lone soul screamed out, "We love your music!"

Rock on, brother. Rock on.

I'm not a musician. And just as a nonmusician girl feels out of place at a musicians' awards event, so will a Best Yes girl feel out of place in a people-pleasing world.

You will sometimes feel exposed. Fidgety. Out of place. Insecure. And oh-so-incredibly awkward. And I want you to understand these feelings aren't a sign that it's time to turn back. Or to give in to that people-pleasing desire beating against your fragile resolve. It's time to say the most important no you'll ever declare.

It's time to say no to yourself. Say to yourself, *I will not let the awkward disappointment of others keep me from my Best Yes appointments with God.*

I will not let the awkward disappointment of others keep me from my Best Yes appointments with God.

APPOINTMENTS AND DISAPPOINTMENTS
WALK HAND IN HAND

Do you know what I wanted to do that night on the red carpet? I wanted to get back in that vehicle. I wanted to go back to the ease of my quiet hotel room. I wanted to rip off that stupid, fancy dress and crawl into bed and pull the covers over my head. I did not want to keep walking that red carpet toward the awards ceremony I was supposed to attend. I did not want to push past that awkward disappointment of the crowd.

But if I was ever going to get where I was supposed to be that night, I was going to have to keep walking forward despite feeling awkward, despite the disappointment of others. And you know what happened once I got inside that awards ceremony? An appointment from God I wouldn't have ever experienced if I'd turned back.

Once inside I found a bathroom. Partly because I wanted to make sure my dress hadn't ripped in embarrassing places when my heel got caught. And partly because when you feel terribly awkward and out of place, bathroom stalls are glorious places to regroup.

When I walked in, there was a girl staring at herself in the mirror. I'm not especially inclined to make small talk, so I walked past her and into a stall. When I came out, she was still there. Still staring.

"You okay?" I asked.

"Not really." At first it was just those two words. But then more. And quickly I realized her heart had been knocked around a bit out on that red carpet too. She was an amazingly talented musician. But her body size had been the topic of one too many hard conversations.

I guess because she didn't know me, she felt like she could open up to me. I wasn't in her music world, but I do personally know the pain of weight struggles. I know how thoughtless comments can cut deeply into a heart. And I know what it feels like to step on that scale and feel like a failure.

We talked. We shared. We laughed. And together we gained just a bit more courage. It was an appointment I wouldn't have experienced if I'd allowed disappointment to scare me away.

Appointments and disappointments walk hand in hand. I had to get past the disappointment of the crowd to receive this appointment from God. I guess the question is this: Are we going to be a yes girl or a Best Yes girl? My ability to say no will determine which kind of yes girl I will be.

SAYING NO TO OURSELVES

One day on my blog I thought it might be good to chat about all this. Why is it so hard to push past the awkwardness of saying no so we can embrace our Best Yes assignments? And the comments came in like a flood.

Tina said,

> I don't think we were designed [to] be fake superhero women . . . Who are we kidding . . . on the outside we look bullet proof, but we all know that girl with the cape is cheating somewhere . . . quality time with her kids? Quiet time? Body of Christ? Bedroom?[1]

Jeanne said,

> Saying "No" . . . means that we value our time, energy, and needs. This is healthy if balanced. But as Christian women it's almost frowned upon. The Christian attitude seems to be that if you're not killing yourself for others then you're not Christian.[2]

Jane said,

> I am retired from teaching elementary art in the public schools—35 wonderful years! People always think art teachers want their stuff that they consider too good to throw away—their trash. I would never say "no I can't use your things." I was always afraid of hurting their feelings. When I retired, I had a truckload of things to get rid of. And I didn't try to give it away to anyone but the trash bin.

I would have saved myself and my sweet husband a lot of work if I had just been honest.[3]

Do you hear the weariness of not pushing through the awkwardness of disappointing some people? Phrases like:

"That girl with the cape is cheating somewhere."

"If you're not killing yourself for others, then you're not Christian."

"I would have saved myself and my sweet husband a lot of work if I had just been honest."

I picture that sweet art teacher and her husband standing in the middle of all that stuff. Old nut cans with plastic lids that someone thought would make the perfect drum. Baby food jars that someone thought would be perfect for sand art. Milk cartons and soda pop pull tabs and pinecones and twisty ties and old magazines. If this stuff had been part of the teacher's planned assignments, they would have been treasures. But they weren't. And since they weren't part of her plan, they just became burdensome extras. And in the end, she wished she'd just pushed past awkward, past the fear of disappointing others, and been graciously honest.

Indeed, it's times like these we need to say no to others. But first we must get good at saying no to ourselves. No to that resistance inside called awkwardness. Let's declare once again, *I will not let the awkward disappointments of others keep me from my Best Yes appointments with God.*

How do we learn to do this? The answer isn't what might bubble to the surface of our minds first. We might think we just need to become more confident. But it goes deeper than that.

It's not a matter of gaining more confidence. It's a matter

of being more certain of our convictions. Confidence is being more certain of our abilities. Conviction is being more certain of God's instructions.

I'm not talking about the way we sometimes use the word *conviction* as a verb—*I'm convicted to wear longer shorts* or *I'm convicted to have more consistent quiet times*. The kind of conviction I'm referring to is a noun—a firm, foundational belief.

With a deep conviction that God's instruction can be trusted, we can learn to graciously push past awkward. One of my favorite verses to quote when I'm having to tell myself not to get caught up in the awkward disappointments of others is Joshua 1:7–9:

> Be strong and very courageous. Be careful to obey all the law my servant Moses gave you; do not turn from it to the right or to the left, that you may be successful wherever you go. Keep this Book of the Law always on your lips; meditate on it day and night, so that you may be careful to do everything written in it. Then you will be prosperous and successful. Have I not commanded you? Be strong and courageous. Do not be afraid; do not be discouraged, for the LORD your God will be with you wherever you go.

Best Yes answers are strong and courageous. Strength and courage come from keeping God's Word close. We'll talk more about this in future chapters. But for now, know that God's Word has to be front and center. We have to be thinking about it, be able to quote it. Refuse to let fear and discouragement hold us back; for wherever we go, God will be with us.

When faced with that awkward fear of disappointment,

pushing past it might just be asking myself, *What is the strong and courageous thing to do here?* For my convictions tell me that God will be with me wherever I go.

Strong and courageous enough to keep walking down that red carpet.

Strong and courageous enough to graciously thank the mom trying to donate dryer lint but explain it's not fitting with our art curriculum.

Strong and courageous enough not to try and fake being a superwoman who can do it all.

Not because I'm more confident in what I can and can't do. But rather because I have a deep conviction of God's instructions for me to be strong and courageous wherever I go, remembering He will be with me.

ACCORDING TO HIS CONVICTIONS

The man who lived those verses above, of course, was Joshua. Listen to how crucial Joshua and Caleb's convictions were in another part of their story. In Joshua 14, we find Caleb reminding Joshua of the reward due to him because of their courage forty years earlier. All those years ago when Moses sent twelve men in to gather information about the promised land, only Caleb and Joshua stood strong so that the land could be taken.

The other ten men "gave Moses this account: 'We went into the land to which you sent us, and it does flow with milk and honey! Here is its fruit. But the people who live there are powerful, and the cities are fortified and very large. We even saw descendants of Anak there'" (Num. 13:27–28).

These ten men were reporting from the vantage point of whether or not they felt confident. When they lacked confidence, they lacked courage, and even more tragically, they lacked faith that God would be with them. When they perceived the people who were occupying the land they were supposed to take were dangerous giants, they didn't feel they had the ability to do the job.

Joshua and Caleb didn't report back based on their confidence but based on their conviction. Though they had seen the exact giants the other ten had seen, their report was very different. Here's how Caleb told the story decades later:

> I was forty years old when Moses the servant of the LORD sent me from Kadesh Barnea to explore the land. And I brought him back a report *according to my convictions*, but my fellow Israelites who went up with me made the hearts of the people melt in fear. I, however, followed the LORD my God wholeheartedly. So on that day Moses swore to me, "The land on which your feet have walked will be your inheritance and that of your children forever, because you have followed the LORD my God wholeheartedly."
>
> Now then, just as the LORD promised, he has kept me alive for forty-five years since the time he said this to Moses, while Israel moved about in the wilderness. So here I am today, eighty-five years old! I am still as strong today as the day Moses sent me out; I'm just as vigorous to go out to battle now as I was then. Now give me this hill country that the LORD promised me that day. You yourself heard then that the Anakites were there and their cities were

large and fortified, but, the LORD helping me, I will drive
them out just as he said. (Josh. 14:7–12, emphasis added)

Did you catch that? Caleb brought back a report *according
to his convictions*. He didn't go along with the crowd. Maybe
he knew going against the other ten spies would be awkward.
Maybe he knew they'd be disappointed not to have him sup-
port their fear-based initiative. But Caleb refused to let the
awkward disappointment of others keep him from his Best Yes
appointments with God.

And though it would take forty-five years to be able to get
to that promised land, Caleb and Joshua were the only ones
from that generation to enter it.

And here's another thing that strikes me in the passages
above. Caleb didn't ache with weariness. Caleb was now
eighty-five years old, saying, "I am still as strong today as I
was when I was forty. I'm just as vigorous to go out to battle
now as I was then" (v. 11).

Maybe he was taking some really good vitamins. Maybe
he had stellar genes. Maybe eighty-five years old in biblical
times didn't feel the same as eighty-five years old today. I don't
know. But here's what I do know: God made a point to tell
us. He thought it was important to note that Caleb still had
strength and vigor all those years later.

I'm sure a theologian could unpack this with mind-blowing
reasoning.

But I just can't help but think it had something to do with
his ability to push past the awkwardness of disappointing others. When I alter my Best Yes decisions because I'm too afraid
to disappoint someone, it wears me out. Saying yes all the time

won't make me Wonder Woman. It will make me a worn-out woman.

Saying yes all the time won't make me Wonder Woman. It will make me a worn-out woman.

Caleb made decisions in line with God's Word. Truth was his conviction—his absolute certainty, his unwavering belief—that God would be with him.

Amazing.

Amazing man.

Amazing conviction.

Amazing Best Yes.

Amazing outcome.

Remember what I said earlier about walking the red carpet? If I was ever going to get where I was supposed to be that night, I was going to have to keep walking forward despite feeling awkward, despite the disappointment of others.

Appointment and disappointment walk hand in hand. To accept one invitation is to decline another. It's time to decide which invitation we're going to accept. Are we going to be a yes girl or a Best Yes girl? A yes girl lets the disappointment of others keep her from making Best Yes decisions.

If Caleb had just been a yes man, he would have gone along with the other spies. He would have negated his instructions from God to be strong and courageous. He would have forgotten that God was with him. He would have made this decision based on his own confidence and not on his conviction.

And he would have never discovered his Best Yes promised land.

Sweet sister, please note this. In between where you are now and where you want to be will usually be a pathway of awkwardness. A crowd of potentially disappointed people. It's your choice to shrink back from your Best Yes or embrace your Best Yes.

As hard as it is to disappoint a person in order to keep your appointment with God, remember on the other side of awkward—for those who choose well—awaits a de-junked classroom with only the necessary supplies, a music awards program with a divine appointment, and a promised land you don't want to miss.

Chapter 13

But What If I Say No and They Stop Liking Me?

LET'S JUST CALL THE ELEPHANT IN THE ROOM WHAT IT is—a massive, dirty, grayish, tusk-adorned, tail-swinging, giant-legged, big-bellied creature with ears that some cartoon creators believe make them able to fly. And it's in our space. We see it. We navigate around it. We let it take up room. But we don't want to acknowledge it.

Still, it's there, stinking up the place, and I want to talk about it.

We dread saying yes but feel powerless to say no. Why? Because of the elephant called *people pleasing*. We talked around the edges of people pleasing in the last chapter, but in this chapter I want to dive right into the heart of the struggle.

We are afraid of people not liking us. Not admiring us. Not being pleased with us. So we spend the best of who we are doing a million things we know we aren't supposed to be doing.

Well, let's usher that elephant out of our living spaces and follow it all the way to where it will take us. Let's run alongside its clunky gait and earth-shattering footsteps. And see what allowing this elephant to be present is really costing us.

Everything.

Why? Because it is impossible to please everyone. And wearing yourself out trying will often make you the unhappiest person in the room.

I once heard a great message from Dr. Howard Hendricks called "Keeping the Elephants Off Your Air Hose." It's been years, possibly decades, since I heard that message, yet I remember that title as if it were yesterday. Why? Because I need to remember it. When an elephant sits on your air hose, you can't breathe. And if you can't breathe, you can't live.

We fear disappointing people. And you know that elephant is sitting on your air hose when you start operating under the assumption it is possible to do enough, give enough, sacrifice enough, and then *surely* everyone will like you. And be pleased with you. And talk nice about you. And name their next child after you.

Welcome to my brand of crazy.

Hello, my name is Lysa, and I want people to like me. I try and try and try to make sure I please them. And it gets me in trouble. Like when an elephant sits on my air hose. Because it is impossible to please everyone.

I think we need to repeat that. Close your eyes, take a long sip of that Diet Coke or grande latte you're drinking, and let this truth sink in as deep as that drink. Take it all the way in. And don't just ingest it. Digest it. Make it part of how you live and how you make decisions.

It is impossible to please everyone.

Take it from a girl who has certainly tried. When my kids were little and I was just starting to travel and speak, some of my fellow mommy friends didn't understand. I sometimes got comments that made me feel very insecure and uncertain. Instead of just discussing their concerns with them, I started trying to reshape their opinions of me. In my mind, I heard them communicating that good moms stayed with their kids 24/7 and bad moms worked outside the home.

I stopped talking about my ministry work and instead wove statements throughout our conversations that lined up with their thinking. When we were together, I verbally painted pictures of my life around what I thought would please them. Make them think I was a good mom. And then they'd like me.

I not only wove these people-pleasing threads into my conversations with other moms, I used them with my family.

My little mantra with the kids was, "You know Mommy's favorite place is at home with you, right?" We'd be sitting on the couch reading, and I'd throw in a quick, "I wouldn't want to be anywhere else in the world except right here with you." And after bath time, I let all the kids pile on my bed for a quick snuggle with Dad and I'd say, "This bed is my favorite place in the world."

I meant those words. I did.

I meant them with everything in me.

But I wasn't just saying them as sweet, reassuring statements for my kids.

I also said them over and over in hopes of my kids repeating them in front of those mommies with opinions. More than once I overheard those other moms asking one of my kids, "Are you sad when your mommy has to go off to work?"

Ouch. It hurts when people corner your kids. I wanted to build a good script into my kids so they'd know with confidence how to respond. Going to work wasn't a proclamation that I preferred work over them. I was just a young mom trying to balance two wonderful callings.

Maybe it was a misguided attempt to shape the opinions of my people so that those mommies who weren't pleased would be pleased. *Ugh.* Why did I care about their opinions so stinkin' much?

What happened next was what you might call a classic mommy backfire, and it was one for the record books, one that I'm sure those mommies are still talking about to this day.

It was Brooke's big "Let's Celebrate Mommy Day" at the church preschool. All the mommies waited excitedly in the hall for little hands to put last-minute touches on the well-decorated room.

I was already feeling out of place as I stood with all the other moms who'd taken time to do their hair and wear outfits. My wet hair was slicked back haphazardly in a banana clip. My black exercise pants had some sort of smear across the thigh. And my tennis shoes looked clunky standing with all the other cute sandals and well-pedicured toes.

Finally, the teacher came to the classroom door and welcomed us inside. A room full of cupcakes, giggles, claps, and sparkling preschool eyes greeted us. The highlight of the room was the clothesline with pinned artistic treasures. Each child had been asked to draw a picture of his or her mommy's favorite place. Then the teacher wrote below the crayon masterpiece what the child said when drawing the picture.

There were pictures of beaches and mountains and even a grocery store. I loved walking down the clothesline and enjoying the preschool artistic expressions of all these fun places. The preciousness abounded. *Until*. Until I got to Brooke's picture featuring my favorite place.

"My mommy's favorite place is in bed with Daddy."

Oh, have mercy on my soul that could have died a thousand deaths right there in the preschool room.

I kid you not. And if I thought my fellow mommies were judging me before, well, let's just say I was not the most invited guest to the mommy playgroups after that.

It is impossible to please everyone.

Am I saying to back out of every situation you find yourself in where you are trying to please someone? No.

TIME TO CHECK OUR HEARTS

While not all pleasing is bad, it can easily be taken to unhealthy extremes. When you have a pattern of saying yes when you know you should say no, it's time to reevaluate some things.

And a good time to reevaluate is now. Before you sign up for something new. Or make another commitment. Or sign your name to that volunteer sheet being passed around. Wait. Think. Take a powerful pause and consider some stuff.

We've already discussed the reality that it's impossible to please everyone. Let me build on that layer with something else even harder to understand. Some people won't be pleased, no matter what.

If the person you are trying so hard not to disappoint will be displeased by a no, they'll eventually be disappointed even if you say yes. Bold, but true.

If the person you are trying so hard not to disappoint will be displeased by a no, they'll eventually be disappointed even if you say yes.

Imagine you say with all honesty and integrity, "I'm so sorry but I can't sign up for that job." Or, "I can't drop everything else and help bail you out." Or, "I can't make fifty-five Rice Krispies treats for tomorrow's end-of-grade party." If they get upset, just step back and think about what's really going on. You said no because saying yes would invite crazy into your life. And you've been telling yourself over and over, *No more crazy.* If they push back when you say no, that's disrespectful on their part. And if you play along, it's dysfunctional on your part.

But let's play out what saying yes to making fifty-five Rice Krispies treats by tomorrow morning could do to you and your family. You'll be in a rush running to the grocery store to get the supplies after dinner. When you get home, everyone is tired, especially your youngest who needs to be put to bed right away. You drop the grocery sacks on the counter and attend to bedtime rituals for the baby. But while you're doing that, the other kids get a little mischievous with the groceries left out.

When you come back to the kitchen, you freak out at what you find. Your older two kids just dumped the only box of Rice Krispies you have in the middle of your kitchen floor—ruining your chance to fulfill your new obligation. But it gets worse, because now as you are standing in the kitchen yelling at the top of your lungs, your husband walks in from work. He looks at you with a look that completely unravels something deep inside. All the good you've invested in the kids today will go unnoticed because of the dark shadow this one crazed moment has cast over it all. But we're not done yet, are we?

Next, you kick the dog's water dish on your way to clean up the mess. Now, for sure, you can't use the cereal on the floor. Not that you'd use cereal from the floor to make stuff for the bake sale in the first place—really. Or maybe you were half thinking about it. Because, oh my gosh, what will Polly Perfect say if you show up empty-handed at the o'dark hundred hour for the class party tomorrow morning?

So you cry. You start scooping Rice Krispies off the floor, trying desperately to pick out the wet clumps from the semiusable cereal. You berate yourself for yelling at the kids. You convince yourself that look your husband gave you means a million awful things. How did life come to this? You feel like such a failure. And you're so very tired of never quite keeping up.

All for what? So a classroom of kids will have sugar at tomorrow's end-of-year class party? So another mom will say thank you and maybe be impressed by your Rice Krispies treats for 5.3 seconds? Now, don't get hung up on the details. It could have gone wrong twenty-seven other ways. The point is that you gave up the peace of your entire family for an unrealistic demand made at an unrealistic hour.

You won't ever be able to keep up with unrealistic. Unrealistic demands lead to undercurrents of failure. So don't allow the unrealistic demands of others to march freely into your life. Resolve instead to make decisions based on what is realistic—not on trying to earn the approval of or impress another.

———

You won't ever be able to keep up with unrealistic. Unrealistic demands lead to undercurrents of failure.

———

It's a vicious cycle, I tell you. Those who constantly try to impress others will quickly depress themselves.

That's not love. In the next chapter we're going to talk about loving others. It's important and it's biblical. But as I said at the very start of this book, we must not confuse the disease to please with the command to love. When someone makes a request of you, you should be able to make that decision without emotional consequences. And if you anticipate that telling them no will make them not like you—then you saying yes isn't going to help that situation. It just won't.

I once volunteered with a woman who was constantly saying, "You know, God is looking for willing women." She would spiritually rationalize that if there are tasks in front of us, we should see them as our assignments. I was so afraid of telling her no. I felt like by doing so I was admitting spiritual weakness and huge deficiencies in my relationship with God.

A couple of times I tried to say no because I had small children, thus making it unrealistic for me to keep the same hours she did. I could tell she wasn't happy. When I asked her about it, she quickly remarked, "I'm so tired of hearing you say that you have small children. We all know you have small children. Don't state the obvious. Just figure out how to make your schedule work."

She wasn't trying to be mean. She wasn't trying to attack me. She was honestly just trying to get a job done based on her deep-down belief that propelled her to think Christian women should please God by absolutely always saying yes to others' requests.

That was a foundational belief in her life. But it was a faulty foundational belief. When she had a need, she sought out a person to fill that need before seeking God first. She left God out of the problem-solving process.

There is a verse that might add some clarity to this discussion: "For the eyes of the LORD range throughout the earth to strengthen those whose hearts are fully committed to him"

(2 Chron. 16:9). Great verse. But taken out of context, we might develop the faulty belief that this is proof the Lord is looking for people who will say yes to everything in front of them. After all, isn't that what "fully committed" means?

No. There is a big difference between saying yes to everyone and saying yes to God. Let's read this verse tucked within the context it's found:

> At that time Hanani the seer came to Asa king of Judah and said to him: "Because you relied on the king of Aram and not on the LORD your God, the army of the king of Aram has escaped from your hand. Were not the Cushites and Libyans a mighty army with great numbers of chariots and horsemen? Yet when you relied on the LORD, he delivered them into your hand. For the eyes of the LORD range throughout the earth to strengthen those whose hearts are fully committed to him. You have done a foolish thing, and from now on you will be at war." (vv. 7–9)

The foolish thing Asa did was relying on the king of Aram instead of the Lord. If we always feel the pressure to be *the answer* to every need and task, we short-circuit others' need to trust God. And like Asa, we will foolishly be at war with this struggle of depending on others over trusting God. So, if I am the person constantly saying yes, I might be hindering others from trusting God. If I am the one always looking to others before depending on God, I need to develop new habits of asking God for His provision and looking for His answers first.

Here's what the commentary in my Bible says about this,

Judah and Israel never learned! Although God had delivered them even when they were outnumbered, they repeatedly sought help from pagan nations rather than from God. That Asa sought help from Aram was evidence of national spiritual decline. With help from God alone, Asa had defeated the Cushites in open battle. But his confidence in God had slipped, and now he sought only a human solution to his problem. When confronted by the prophet Hanani, Asa threw him in prison, revealing the true condition of his heart. It is not sin to use human means to solve our problems, but it is sin to trust them more than God, to think they are better than God's ways, or to leave God completely out of the problem-solving process.[1]

When commenting on these verses, Matthew Henry said, "God is displeased when he is distrusted, and when an arm of flesh is relied on, more than his power and goodness. It is foolish to lean on a broken reed, when we have the Rock of ages to rely upon. . . . We trust in God when we have nothing else to trust to, when need drives us to him; but when we have other things to stay on, we are apt to depend too much on them."[2]

Again, we don't need to take this to such an extreme that we never step in to help people—or that we never have people depend on us, or that we never serve, or that we never fulfill tasks that are before us. If God has put an assignment to serve, give, and help in front of us, He will give us what we need to fulfill that assignment. And through serving in that way, we will be refreshed and refueled.

Being resistant to serving and helping is not at all what I'm saying. What I'm talking about is letting people depend on us to such an extreme that we become their every answer.

Lori said this on my blog,

> Somehow I seem to have turned the meaning of Galatians 6:2 (Carry each other's burdens, and in this way you will fulfill the law of Christ) into a Messiah complex, i.e., symbolically speaking, "I am the Messiah and I gotta carry it for them." This totally misconstrues the meaning of the verse. I am slowly learning to take these burdens to the Lord and allow Him to minister in ways that *I* cannot. It's amazing the weight that is lifted when you allow yourself the ability to say "no."[3]

At the end of the day, a healthy relationship isn't void of service. Of course we must serve, love, give, be available, help, and contribute to the greater good. But we must have the freedom to say yes or no responsibly without fear of emotional consequences.

So far we've talked about two realities: First, it's impossible to please everyone. Second, some people won't be pleased even if we say yes to them. But there's one more reality we should discuss before ending this chapter. You see, it's not just others needing something from us that drives our people-pleasing tendencies. It's also about our needs from them.

ATTACHING PRESUMPTIONS TO PROMISES

People make requests of us because they need something from us. And we've discussed how unhealthy it can be when we say yes because we don't know how to say no or we fear saying no. But we also say yes in times when we should say no because we're trying to get a need met as well. We should really listen to our own thoughts when making decisions.

If I find myself saying, "If I do this, then they will [*not make me feel badly for saying no* or *like me* or *do something for me* or *owe me a favor* or *make me feel accepted*]," then I'm not just giving an answer. I'm promising to do something while making the presumption I'll also get something. I'm attaching strings to my reason for saying yes.

Promises with strings of presumption attached will set both people up for disappointment. We need to answer requests without secretly making requests. I need to be able to say yes to something without presuming this yes will make a way for me to feel more, have more, or have more owed to me. And I need to say no without presuming this no will make me feel less, have less, or be owed less.

Time for a little pushback, right? I mean, isn't some of this natural relationship currency? After all, I made the bed this morning hoping to make my husband happy. I agreed to watch my friend's kids for her knowing she's always so willing to do the same for me. I made plans to spend time with my aunt in a couple of weeks because I don't want her to be alone for her birthday. I know doing these things keeps these relationships healthy, which means they'll be mutually beneficial to all involved.

Here's the difference: these situations are examples of mutual giving, not manipulative gain. They are acts of kindness and love without strings of presumptive payback attached.

Remember, relationships don't fit in neat boxes. Often the

best ones slop over the edges of neat and normal. That's okay. This chapter wasn't meant to make you start doubting all your interactions and determining that everyone you know has issues.

Take all this and ponder it, friend. Determine to use it to move some of your relationships forward or put the brakes on others. But in the midst of it all, challenge yourself to be honest about what's really going on with all those requests and invitations and opportunities.

The sooner we can make peace with the facts we can't please everyone and some people won't be pleased no matter what, the sooner we can be freed from that elephant sitting on our air hose. We'll have the oxygen and the energy to simply and generously love. After all, love, real love, is a very Best Yes.

Chapter 14

A Best Yes Is Seen by Those Who Choose to See

THE OTHER DAY I WAS IN A DRIVE-THRU EARLY IN THE morning. (Please note, I was by myself this time. I have gotten smart about how to pull off this drive-thru thing since the beginning of the book.) I wanted to surprise my daughter with one of her favorite biscuits. This eating establishment makes them every morning—golden brown on the top and bottom, fluffy in the middle, and good and buttered all around.

It's the kind of thing one can enjoy in the teen years. I'm at the age where I must avoid said items. It's sad but true.

What's also sad but true is the reason I had to get her biscuit at the drive-thru restaurant instead of just making biscuits at home. The ones I sometimes bake from popped-open cans shame the country-cooking roots from which my people came. The women in my lineage handled a rolling pin as if it were a third arm. I don't even own a rolling pin. I don't think.

So my girl would be absolutely thrilled at this restaurant-bought, real biscuit.

I ordered it and grabbed my wallet for the necessary two dollars.

Two dollars isn't a big deal until you need it and don't have it. I scrambled through my purse, then the middle console of my car, and then in all the places change might have fallen. Nothing. I then decided I'd just use a credit card. Which would have been an amazing plan if only my credit card had been where it was supposed to be in my wallet.

That's when I got completely desperate and started praying for the person in front of me to please feel some sort of divine nudge to pay for my order. Maybe? Please?

But at the very last minute there was no need for that nudge. As I pulled up to the window, I found my credit card wrapped up in a receipt at the bottom of my purse. Biscuit saved.

As I handed my credit card through the window, I had the strangest notion to use that desperate feeling in an act of obedience. *Don't waste it. Let it make you aware. Be an extension of God's love right now.*

So I paid for the breakfast of the guy behind me. That's nothing new, right? But don't miss the point here. I don't want to focus on the act of paying for food. It's the revelation of paying attention.

Paying attention to what's in front of us will help us see our Best Yes. I saw what it felt like to need someone to pay for my breakfast, so I used it as a Best Yes. Not that every responsibility is our responsibility—we've already talked plenty about that.

I mean, I didn't walk into the restaurant and buy everyone's breakfast. I just simply and quietly gave to the guy behind me.

I think this is the way Best Yes things often unfold. We want big directional signs from God. God just wants us to pay attention.

We want big directional signs from God. God just wants us to pay attention.

CHOOSING OUR BEST YES

The other day my friend Meredith was trying to make a simple decision. Should she stay home to spend time with her husband or go to her weekly get-together with friends? She was feeling torn between two good choices. Which was her Best Yes?

I challenged Meredith to simply pay attention to what was right in front of her. Had she seen indications that she and her husband needed a night together? Or had she seen that she needed to have some girl time and the invigorating conversation with friends? What had she seen as the strongest indication right in front of her lately?

Pay attention to that.

Her husband had been out of town. She sensed she needed to be home with him. She paid attention and invested in her marriage. She became an extension of God's love to her husband.

That was a Best Yes. And we will see our Best Yes answers

most clearly when we are present, paying attention, seeing what we need to see, and being willing to extend God's love in the moment.

We've talked a lot about saying no in this Best Yes book. And I understand how that rubs against the grain of what some of us are used to. There might be an inner hesitation saying, "It's not Christian to reject people! Don't you dare say no."

Saying no isn't an unnecessary rejection. It's actually a necessary protection of our Best Yes answers. My friend Jud Wilhite told me recently he has to say no to some of the never-ending tasks at his church. That's hard for a pastor to do. But he knows he must protect some of his time and energy for his family. He said, "When I tell someone no, I visualize my family and see myself saying yes to them." I love that.

Saying no isn't an unnecessary rejection. It's actually a necessary protection of our Best Yes answers.

We will have a very hard time paying attention to those Best Yes answers if we live lives that are completely spent. Instead, why not completely spend yourself on the assignments that are yours, those moments you shouldn't dare miss, the calling that pulses in your soul, the love you and only you can offer?

Bob Goff, the craziest lawyer, love activist, world-changer I know, and the delightful author of *Love Does*, says this:

The world can make you think that love can be picked up at a garage sale or enveloped in a Hallmark card. But the kind of love that God created and demonstrated is a costly one because it involves sacrifice and presence. It's a love that operates more like a sign language than being spoken outright. . . . The brand of love Jesus offers is . . . more about presence than undertaking a project. It's a brand of love that doesn't just think about good things, or agree with them, or talk about them . . . Love does.[1]

Did you catch what Bob said? It's "more about presence than undertaking a project." I agree. We can't just say yes because there's a project to be done. We have to say a Best Yes to the presence only we can offer. Be present in your life, right where you are, and dare to look. Look for the little everyday answers to decisions you have to make by being fully present.

And that act of "being present" will take you places. Some of those places will be no farther than the end of the drive-thru line with a biscuit in tow or a date on the couch talking with your husband. But then other Best Yes answers will send you on a wild and wonderful adventure.

BE PRESENT

I was present when in the third grade my teacher brought her husband into our classroom. He worked for a newspaper. He got paid to write words. I tucked that in my heart. Then one day my dad brought a typewriter home. I walked up to that amazing machine that clacked and clicked and dinged and zipped. I placed my hands on it and thought, *One day when*

I know enough words, I will write a book to help other people.
I would celebrate many birthdays and witness the extinction
of the typewriter before that dream came into being. But it
started the day I was present in the third grade.

I was present on a phone call one day when my mother-in-
law mentioned that crisis pregnancy centers offer post-abortion
counseling. Something seized in me. I needed that help. I went.
I received tender love, forgiveness, help, and hope. I then became a counselor at that center to love on terrified girls and be
that voice that says, "I truly understand."

Eventually, after years of healing and only telling scared
girls in counseling rooms my story, I stood before a small gather-
ing of women at a church. With trembling knees and a cracking
voice, I shared my story. What I didn't realize was that many of
those women had also had abortions; but since no one else was
talking about it, they kept their secrets, and dark shame ate away
at their hearts. I went first. And then they could be brave too.
Being present to the hope my mother-in-law gave me eventually
allowed me to extend it to many, many hurting women.

I was present at a quick lunch meeting one day that led to
what is now Proverbs 31 Ministries. It was just two moms in
ponytails and sweatpants. With newborns in baby carriers we
dared to ask the question, "What if other women like us need
encouragement?" Almost twenty years later, close to a million
women a day engage with words of encouragement and truth
that go out from Proverbs 31 Ministries.

I was present at a breakfast last summer at a family camp.
A lady asked if she might sit with me. Somehow we got on the
subject of handling criticism. I shared with her about a harsh
letter I'd received and how I was working through trying to
see what was true and what I just needed to forgive and let go.

This week I received an e-mail from that lady thanking me. She'd received a similar letter just recently, one that might have crushed her had it not been for the remembrance that I'd gotten one too. She wasn't alone. And just knowing that helped her.

I was present when my church needed someone to serve with gifts that I have. My heart soars when I go to these meetings and use my talents and resources for the body of Christ. I am also present in my commitment to be a voice of encouragement to my church staff. Each week I send a note, text, or tweet to someone who works hard to make our church what it is. Jesus is passionate about us serving and giving to our local churches. Yes, I'm involved with an outside ministry, but staying connected on deep levels with my home church is crucially important.

I was present last night when my daughter needed to go get ice cream. With a million other things pressing in on me, I knew in that moment she was my Best Yes. So, we hopped in the car and sang obnoxiously loud along with the radio. We let our hair get tangled up in the wind and our hearts with each other. We didn't have any kind of deep and meaningful conversation. We were just present with each other. I loved her and she loved me. And it was great.

I brought to each of those encounters my presence and my love, my Best Yes. And one Best Yes after another took me places I'd have never had the privilege to go if I hadn't dared to look at what was right in front of me.

I'm not saying, *Yay me!* Heavens, for every time I was present in my life there were probably fifteen misses. But those I caught, those moments I was present? Amazing. Maybe you feel like you've missed more than you've caught. Maybe this small answer of being present is doing nothing but creating more questions for you. That's okay. That's actually fantastic. That's you being present. Right here. Right now.

Bob Goff goes on to say in the epilogue of *Love Does*:

> Let me tell you what I do when I don't know what to do to move my dreams down the road. I usually just try to figure out what the next step is and then do that. I know it sounds too simple, too formulaic; it seems like there must be more to it. But there isn't. For most of us, that next step is as easy as picking up the phone, sending an e-mail, writing a letter, buying a plane ticket, or just showing up. After that, things start happening. Things that perhaps have God's fingerprints on them. You'll know which ones do and which ones don't. Pick the ones that do.[2]

I love that Bob recognized there will be dos and don'ts. *Pick the ones that do.*

The other day I posted a question through social media and asked, "What's a decision you're having a hard time making right now?" The decisions that needed to be made overwhelmed me. There were so many.

Decisions about whether to stay in a job or pursue the ministry.

Decisions about relationships and forgiveness and breakups and makeups.

Decisions about colleges and kids and infertility and adoption.

Decisions about whether this is God saying no or Satan just trying to get in the way.

Decisions about finances and moving and hard-to-deal-with family members.

So many decisions.

I took this one small thought of simply being present and dared to whisper it over many of those decisions. I just wanted to see if this thought of "being present" could hold up under the litmus test of everyday life. And I think it does. In each of those situations, being present with a heart bent toward love and daring to look at what's been placed right in front of you is honestly the best place to start.

Look at what you do know. Look at that very next step. Or, as Bob says, that next call, that next e-mail, that next visit.

Refuse to get all tangled up and held back by what you don't know. And most of all, know who you want to be and take the next step that points you in the direction of that character quality. Abe Lincoln has been quoted as saying, "I don't know who my grandfather was, and am more concerned to know what his grandson will be."[3] There's a Best Yes attitude for sure.

Who do you want to be? I want to be like the most nonfrantic woman my family ever met, a woman who knows the gentle art of a life brush-stroked with her Best Yes, a woman who knows how to be lovingly present.

THE MOST NONFRANTIC WOMAN I'D EVER MET

She was knocking at my front door trying to balance her paper coffee cup, her purse, her cell phone, and a stack of papers. She was also trying to fix something on her shoe. She hopped a step or two when I answered the door.

I smiled. Her imperfect posture delighted my mind that had been feeling a little off-kilter all morning. She smiled back and hopped one more time.

Finally whatever was bugging her with her shoe seemed fixed. She stood up and smiled with an apologetic smile that made me adore her before we'd ever had our first conversation.

She spent all day with my family and me. She was a reporter doing a story on our sons adopted from Africa. Even though she never alluded to another title she had, we knew. She was the daughter of a former president of the United States. As in she and her sister called the White House their home at one time. Her mom had been the First Lady, which made her part of the First Family. But that wasn't her role that day. She was a reporter. She was at our house to do a story. She stayed present in that role alone.

Her questions were honest and unassuming, her demeanor kind, her laugh delightfully loud, her paperwork messy, but her focus clear. She was there to uncover a story, to write a string of words to tell a story. That day was about the story.

She stayed focused on the task at hand. She wasn't encumbered with a thousand other things pulling at her. She didn't try to multitask too much. She wasn't a slave to her cell phone. She wasn't running late or running from one thing to the next. She said no to everything else pulling at her so she could say yes to the story. She gave it her Best Yes.

At the writing of this, I have no idea how well the story will turn out. But this woman who demonstrated a Best Yes that day left a lasting impression on my family for sure. Later at dinner, Art asked the kids to go around the table and say one word to describe the reporter.

"Nice."

"Humble."

"Classy."

"Elegant."

"Humble."

Then there may or may not have been an awesome little exchange from an older sibling to the youngest child: "You can't say humble. I just said humble. You always want to copy what I have to say!"

I love family bonding.

But I really love the collective experience of this nonfrantic woman. And the words my kids used to describe her.

Art went on to ask the kids to explain what she did and how she carried herself that led us to use such great words to describe her. Then he turned the conversation on each of us.

"If you want people to use such great words to describe you, think about the decisions you are making. How are they leading people to describe you?"

Great descriptions are birthed from great decisions. The decisions we make, make the lives we live. If we want to live better, we've got to decide better. *Yes* and *No.* The two most powerful words.

Yes and No.
The two most powerful words.

And a soul well-spent will be one who lives Best Yes answers: The wife spending time with her husband. Bob the lawyer being a love activist. The reporter being focused and humble and classy. And you—are you ready now to dare to look at and extend God's love to what's right there and give it your Best Yes?

Chapter 15

The Thrill of an Unrushed Yes

EACH MORNING I HAVE A ROUTINE WITH MY HUSBAND. It's simple. Nothing profound. Nothing for which we'd ever stop and snap a picture. It's just a moment. He asks me to help him pick a tie. He then goes away to fuss with this fixture of his professional job. Soon he returns with a flipped-up collar and a pressed-down, knotted tie. He needs gentle hands to fold the collar over. Actually, he doesn't need. He wants gentle hands to fold the collar over. And I do.

It's just a moment.

But it's a moment when we follow the "excellent way" of love. In the intersection of this unrushed moment, we're once again saying to each other: I love you. I love you too.

Please don't get an overly idyllic picture in your head of our marriage. Heavens, no. We have plenty of those "growth opportunity" moments too. But this moment with the tie, it's like a spot of glue ever tightening the bond between us day by day. It's so simple, and yet something I would miss with the deepest ache imaginable if today were the last of the moments.

If today.

Tears slip as I think about this. Dear God, help me think about this. Let me snap a hundred of these moments with the lens of my heart to be stored and appreciated and thought of as the great treasures they are.

Let my mind park there. Let my heart relish there. Let my mouth dare to whisper what a joy this is. I love you. I love us. I love this moment each day.

Our relationship isn't perfect; no relationship is perfect. We're two very strong-willed people with vastly different approaches to life. And, oh, how easy it would be to list all the differences. He likes the towel hanging in the same spot. I am more creative. But I stop the list there.

I stop because great love isn't two people finding the perfect match in each other. Great love is two people making the choice to be a match. A decision. To fold his collar and snap the heart lens and find myself grateful to the point of tears. Tears of relishing today are so much better than tears of regret.

It's just a moment together.

Or is it?

This kind of together can only happen when we choose to experience the thrill of an unrushed yes. It's being together and relishing that togetherness even with all its imperfections. This is true for marriages but also for family and for friends who feel like family.

This beautifully messy band of people I call my own needs

time together. Space to connect and process. Conversational threads are what make up the fabric of relationships. We must take time. Make time. To be together. To connect. To talk.

And this isn't natural to me. I'm a task girl. I like accomplishing things. I like the thrill of moving forward, creating momentum, and getting stuff done.

But the more I choose to pause and talk and really connect, the more I discover the thrill in the sacred spaces of relationships. Leaving room in my life for the unrushed yes strengthens the fabric of my relationships so they can better withstand the wear and tear of everyday life.

And even more, giving priority to relationships does something good in my soul. My soul needs to resist the rush. I love what my friend Ann Voskamp says, "Rushing is for amateurs." I agree. But I don't always live like I agree. I need to be reminded that my soul needs time for relationships.

Honestly, can you imagine how crazy rushed we'd be if we only had tasks to do but not people with whom we must pause to connect? When my kids were little, I used to make the mistake of thinking about how much more I would be able to get done when they were a little older. And then I'd even go so far as to think I'd be less stressed when I had the freedom to spend more time accomplishing the tasks at hand.

But that hasn't proven true. My kids are teenagers now. I do have more time available to me, but that doesn't naturally reduce my stress. Why? Because I have taken on more and more tasks. Instead of keeping the same number of tasks and having more time to accomplish those, I've just added more and more.

Oh, how we live in an age of extreme multitasking, right?

But here's a little cautionary thought. Checking your e-mail in the middle of creative work momentarily knocks your IQ down ten points, according to the British Institute of Psychiatry. The research shows that our brains aren't wired for multi-tasking. One author called it "junk food for the brain."[1]

Well, if too many simultaneous tasks are like junk food for our brains, then I think relationships can help. Hebrews 10:24–25 reminds us to "consider how we may spur one another on toward love and good deeds, not giving up meeting together, as some are in the habit of doing, but encouraging one another—and all the more as you see the Day approaching."

Connecting with those we love is like soul food. It's not that we don't have tasks to do, but rather that we don't fill up with tasks at the risk of starving our relationships. Relationships nourish us in ways nothing else can. It's the relationships that help unrush us.

Relationships can complicate things. But they also have the power to force us into a much simpler rhythm.

I understand the hesitation that some relationships are the very things that drain us. Be smart and honest about the relationships to which you give your time. But we must be careful, if we've gotten burned by a few, that we don't lump all relationships into the hard category. Get smart with whom you spend your time. But do take this time.

Yes, all relationships require work. And yes, relationships can complicate things. But they also have the power to force us into a much simpler rhythm. Stop. Listen. Talk. Process. Walk. Notice. Engage. Compliment. Thank. Hold hands. Just be together.

Last year my then-thirteen-year-old daughter tweeted her to-do list. I was profoundly challenged by how she set her priorities. In between her reminders to print her social studies report, take her allergy medicine, and "take shower, hair looks bad" line items, she listed other things of great importance:

- Tell Mom you love her.
- Thank Jesus for being there for you.
- Give Daddy a hug.
- Tell Ashley she is a great big sister.
- Tell Hope she looks really pretty.

Now, granted, she's only thirteen. And her list of responsibilities doesn't compare to yours or mine. But one day it will. And I love that she's practicing the unrushed yes now. She is preserving and protecting and paving the road for good life relationships.

"MOSES, WHAT YOU'RE DOING ISN'T GOOD"

There's an interesting story in the Old Testament where Jethro, Moses' father-in-law, had to step in and help Moses unrush a season of his life.

In Exodus 18:7–12, we find a sweet reunion between Jethro

and Moses. It even says Moses went out to meet his father-in-law and kissed him. Then they sat together for a good long while and talked. I know it was a good long while because verse 8 says, "Moses told his father-in-law about everything the Lord had done to Pharaoh and the Egyptians for Israel's sake and about all the hardships they had met along the way and how the Lord had saved them."

And I know there was a loving trust in this relationship because Moses trusted Jethro enough to even talk about the hardships they met along the way. You know you don't talk about your mess with just anybody. From what I can tell, Moses and Jethro had a good relationship. They got all caught up on the current state of affairs in Moses' world, and Jethro was delighted about all the Lord had done. He even ended the night with a burnt offering and sacrifices with Moses and all the elders of Israel.

I've read this story so many times in the last couple of days because what happens next challenges me on several levels. Let's read the passage together. I know it's long, but stick with me and I'll unpack it at the end.

> The next day Moses took his seat to serve as judge for the people, and they stood around him from morning till evening. When his father-in-law saw all that Moses was doing for the people, he said, "What is this you are doing for the people? Why do you alone sit as judge, while all these people stand around you from morning till evening?"
>
> Moses answered him, "Because the people come to me to seek God's will. Whenever they have a dispute, it

is brought to me, and I decide between the parties and inform them of God's decrees and instructions."

Moses' father-in-law replied, "What you are doing is not good. You and these people who come to you will only wear yourselves out. The work is too heavy for you; you cannot handle it alone. Listen now to me and I will give you some advice, and may God be with you. You must be the people's representative before God and bring their disputes to him. Teach them his decrees and instructions, and show them the way they are to live and how they are to behave. But select capable men from all the people—men who fear God, trustworthy men who hate dishonest gain—and appoint them as officials over thousands, hundreds, fifties and tens. Have them serve as judges for the people at all times, but have them bring every difficult case to you; the simple cases they can decide themselves. That will make your load lighter, because they will share it with you. If you do this and God so commands, you will be able to stand the strain, and all these people will go home satisfied."

Moses listened to his father-in-law and did everything he said. He chose capable men from all Israel and made them leaders of the people, officials over thousands, hundreds, fifties and tens. (Ex. 18:13–25)

So here's what challenges me deeply—Moses didn't resist Jethro. The Scriptures say that "Moses listened to his father-in-law and did *everything* he said" (emphasis added). I think it would have been hard for a leader like Moses to just have his father-in-law pop in and suddenly say, "What you are doing is not good." Excuse me, Jethro? And you're not even going to soften your criticism by telling me first all you see I'm doing right?

Yeah, I'm challenged by how well Moses responded to Jethro. But here's what I think preceeded Jethro's challenge that helped it go so well—relationship. Jethro was a spiritual father to Moses. They'd connected together. They'd shared together. They'd processed together. They'd sacrificed together. They'd eaten together.

And Moses tasted more than just roasted meat during his meal with Jethro. He tasted the sweetness of a soul satisfied with a good relationship. Jethro wasn't just giving Moses a better way to lead the people. He was giving Moses a better way for them all to resist the constant strains and embrace the unrushed yes of protecting their relationships.

Dividing out the responsibilities of settling issues would provide more white space for Moses and quicker answers for the people. Remember, this wasn't just for Moses. Jethro said to Moses, "What you are doing is not good. *You and these people* who come to you will only wear yourselves out . . ." It was for Moses and the people with whom he had relationships.

In other words, do what you need to do to protect and strengthen the fabric of your relationships. It is okay to get help. Divide up your responsibilities. And if you don't have any way to get help, then reduce your task list. Do what you need to do to have healthy relationships.

Absolutely, the unrushed yes strengthens the fabric of my relationships so they can better withstand the wear and tear of everyday life. But it also provides space to recognize when relationships need extra attention, extra investments so things don't unravel.

THE UNRAVELING OF A MARRIAGE

I had a favorite sweater I loved wearing. It wasn't too bulky but was still warm and cozy. The only problem was the threads were loosely woven together. It would snag on things, so I had to be ever so careful when I wore it.

I was always mindful of the delicate nature of this sweater so I could protect it, make it last, and enjoy wearing it time and again.

Until one day I was in a hurry. I grabbed some things I needed for a meeting and rushed to my car. I tossed all my stuff over to the passenger seat, including a spiral notebook. A spiral notebook whose metal-binding wire was caught on my sleeve. As I pulled my arm toward the steering wheel, the notebook came with it and pulled a huge snag in my sweater.

I unhooked myself and assessed the damage.

What I should have done was take the sweater off, put something else on, and later taken the time to repair the snag the correct way. But in the rush of all I had going on, I made the tragic decision to do what seemed easiest in the moment. I snipped the loose threads and hoped for the best. That tragic decision started an unraveling process that ended the life of that beautiful sweater.

A few days ago my husband and I got into an argument. In front of the kids. Over something insignificant. Right before we were about to head out the door to go on a date.

In the heat of the argument, he announced the date was off. He no longer wanted to go. And honestly, I no longer wanted to go either. I wanted to go sit in a coffee shop by myself and make a mental list of all the reasons I was right.

All the reasons he was wrong. And justify my perspective. But it's at this exact moment of resistance that an unraveling can begin.

Doing what seems easy in the moment often isn't what's best for the long term. I pushed for us to still go on our date. It wasn't fun. It wasn't easy. There were tears. There were awkward stretches of silence. But we pushed through the resistance we both felt and eventually talked.

Talking through the snags. The pulls. The things that threaten to unravel us. There is a delicate nature to marriage. Honestly, there's a delicate nature to all relationships. It's so easy to forget that. It's so easy to take it all for granted and stop being careful. Stop being mindful. Stop being protective. Stop and embrace the unrushed yes of investing in those we love. The unraveling can happen so quickly.

My unrushed yes that day led me to apologize. By admitting I was wrong and asking for forgiveness. Repairing the snags the right way—tying a knot and tucking it back into the weave of our relationship fabric.

Conversational threads are what make up the fabric of relationships. We must take time—make time—to talk.

Isn't it funny that when we get married it's called "tying the knot"? For us, this wasn't just an act at the altar.[2] It's something we have to do over and over again.

All relationships require this tying of the knot in one way or another. And all that weaving together of lives happens when we give an unrushed yes to connecting with others. As I said before, conversational threads are what make up the fabric of relationships. We must take time—make time—to talk.

Where do we find this unrushed yes? We make it. We make time for relationships by thinking about them when scheduling our lives. Like Louie Giglio said, "Whenever you say yes to something, there is less of you for something else. Make sure your yes is worth the less."

I don't want my relationships to be what constantly get my less. So I get intentional about leaving enough unscheduled times on my calendar for relationship moments to happen. I must leave space and look for opportunities to give an unrushed yes.

I just want to make sure I leave that sacred space for relationships.

Leave space for dinners around the sticky farm table.
Leave space for friendships less pixilated by getting off
    the computer and getting more face-to-face time.
Leave space for laughter and loud singing on car rides
    long or short.
Leave space for the times my marriage gets snagged and I
    need to tie the knot all over again.
Leave space for the to-do lists to prioritize people, not
    just projects.
Leave space for the talks and walks and the crazy inside
    jokes.
Leave space for folding his collar over his tie.
Leave space for the unrushed yes.

Chapter 16

The Panic That Keeps You from Your Best Yes

I STOOD ON THE EDGE OF THE POOL SUCKING MY STOMACH in. I looked over at my sister who was maybe four or five at the time. She was splashing on the steps leading to the shallow end.

I'm done with the shallow end, I thought. *I'm nine years old. I'm very grown and old enough to know to suck my stomach in and jump into the deep end.*

I pushed past the tangle of reservations. Those less brave, less assured feelings. And jumped. The cold water enveloped me. Swallowed me whole. I let my body fall all the way until my toes touched the bottom. And from the deep, deep bottom I tilted my head back up from where I'd come and blew out a long string of bubbles to keep the water from going in my nose. As the bubbles cleared, I opened my eyes and saw the cloudy small figure of a girl standing on the edge of the deep end.

190

I couldn't see the details of her face. And her figure danced this way and that as the movements of the water distorted the edges of her small frame. But still I knew it was the girl in the pink-and-green flowered bathing suit. My sister.

I pushed through the weight of the water enough for my head to emerge on the surface. "What are you doing? You know you have to stay in the shallow end," half stating, half scolding her.

She wanted to jump. She wanted to swim. She wanted to be old and brave like me. She wanted the thrill of the deep end.

"No." I loved the feeling of bossing her around. As the word formed in my mouth and I found the right tone to convey this one-word warning, I felt in charge. I wanted to keep her safe. That was part of it. But even more I loved this rare moment of authority.

Until I realized she had no intention of listening to me. She taunted me as she pretended like she was going to jump. She swung her arms and bent her body. Her small teeth gritted like all her strength was about to explode out of the bottom of her feet. But at the last moment the edges of her mouth turned upward in a giant smile as she backed away from the pool's side.

I breathed a huge sigh of relief.

I was brave but also realistic. I knew I could keep myself alive in the deep end but seriously doubted I had the strength to keep us both afloat.

Each hot day when we showed up at the pool, we walked to our respective places. Me to the edge of the deep end with a sucked-in stomach and an ever-growing, brave heart. My sister to the stairs in the shallow end. But as the summer went on, I wondered, *Could I? Should I? Bring her out here to the deep?*

Each day I took a second before jumping into the really

fun waters to glance her way. I felt badly for my sister. She didn't know the exhilarating feeling of swimming with the bottom nowhere near her toes. I couldn't just tap my toes on the prickly pool floor to push my head to the surface for air. I had to swim. Tread water. Use my own strength to stay alive. I wanted her to have this feeling.

One day it occurred to me there was more than one way to let her try out the deep end. She didn't have to jump there. I could ease her there. I could let her get on my back and half walk, half bounce down that slope between the shallow and the deep. I could go slowly. And if that next step deeper freaked her out, I could simply back up to where she felt comfortable.

Honestly, I was so impressed with my brilliance. I swam to the shallow end and unveiled my plan as if I were giving my sister the greatest gift one human could bestow on another.

Surprisingly, she was hesitant. *What? How can this be? I just knew she'd leap onto my back and demand I go faster, faster, faster to the deep end!* Nope. It took great convincing on my part and lots of promises not to go any farther than where she felt safe.

Finally, she got on my back and wrapped her arms around my shoulders. I walked slowly to the slope. One baby step down. Two steps. Three.

At the third step, I perched up on the very tip of my toes, suddenly realizing if I took another step, we'd go underwater. The water was already over my chin, right at my nose. I hoisted my sister up to get her a little farther on top of the water.

And I slipped.

We both went under very suddenly. My sister's hands slipped from my shoulders to my throat. It was as if she believed the only way she could be saved was to hold my throat with an increasingly intense amount of strength. Her grip tightened to the point where even when I finally pushed up above the surface, no air could get in. My mind got foggy very quickly, and suddenly I couldn't figure out which way to go to find safety. I became less and less sure of most things around me, but absolutely sure about one thing. I was drowning. And based on the way my sister was frantically kicking her legs and squeezing my throat, so was she.

And here's the craziest part of the story. I can't remember how we were saved. I know we were. My sister and I are both alive today. But I can't remember the rest of the story.

I remember the drowning part in great clarity. I have dreams about it sometimes. I feel the choking sensation and sit straight up in bed, gasping for air and pulling small, imaginary hands away from my throat. But even the dream stops at the point of drowning and not at the point of being saved.

Maybe it's because I'm supposed to have the richest memories of that feeling of panic. And the realization that panic never helps save anyone. If anything, it only impedes whoever does try to help. It's important for me to remember this because I can still find myself in drowning situations.

DROWNING IN INSECURITIES

People can drown in things besides water. People can go under and feel that they can't get back on top. People sometimes slip to the bottom and need to be rescued.

You know where I see this drowning without water and a subsequent panicked response most often? A woman's insecurities. It takes courage to step into this Best Yes mind-set.

It takes courage to say no. It takes courage to say yes. It takes courage to change the unhealthy patterns of our decision making. And anytime we need to be courageous, our deepest insecurities can make us want to back down from change.

Wait, don't stop reading. I have a feeling you are tempted to do that right now. You may see that word, *insecurity*, and determine you aren't insecure, so all I'm about to share with you doesn't apply. But it does. I guarantee you've felt the choking effects of insecurity even if you don't call it that. Thoughts like these:

> *You're not as talented or smart or experienced as she is,*
> *   therefore this new project won't ever really take off.*
> *Your kids just demonstrated every inadequacy you have as*
> *   a mom.*
> *Protect yourself and your dignity. Don't dare try this new*
> *   venture.*
> *If only you were as organized or intentional or creative as*
> *   they are, then maybe you could accomplish this. But the*
> *   reality is, you're not.*
> *Do you see what he just said about you? He knows you*
> *   better than anyone, so if he thinks that, it's true.*
> *This relationship won't ever get any better.*
> *You know this is never going to work, right?*

How do I know you feel these things? Because I don't just observe these in others. I experience these myself.

You may also be tempted to stop reading right now because you are well aware of your struggle with insecurities and you're tired of hearing advice that just makes you feel worse. Statements like: "Get over it" or "Insecurity is just pride turned inward."

Ouch. The last thing I need when choking with insecurities is someone standing off to the side and adding *pride* to my list of issues. I know I have issues. That's why I feel so insecure. Thank you very much and have a nice day. That's like telling a person drowning to just swim harder. Gracious, I know they wish they could.

That drowning feeling? I feel it when a situation or a person exposes those raw places where I feel so limited. Incapable. Unaccepted. Just like in that pool all those years ago, I can go from standing securely with my head above water to slipping down a slope with seemingly nothing to grab hold of. Then the insecurity, always kind of present on my shoulder, slips into a death grip around my throat.

My insecurities grip to the point where nothing life giving can get in. I forget truth. I feel like backing out of relationships. I don't even want to go to church. I know I need these things just as I knew I needed air that day in the pool. But the grip around my throat is too tight. My mind gets foggy very quickly, and suddenly I can't figure out which way to go to find safety. I become less and less sure of most things around me, but absolutely sure about one thing.

I'm drowning.

That's the thing about insecurity. When it grips us, the very thing we need most—truth—is the very thing we have a hard time grasping. There is a sad and startling statistic about drowning: almost half of all drownings occur less than eighty inches from safety.[1] I can be close to truth but still be drowning with my insecurities. I can have truth sitting on my nightstand. I can have it preached to me on Sundays. I can have truth sent to me through the You Version Bible app. Yes, life-saving truth can be so very close. But grasping on to it and standing on it and letting it shift my thinking away from panic—that's something that requires truth to be more than just close.

That requires truth to be inside me, guiding me, rewiring my thinking, and whispering, "Safety is right here. Insecurity will stop choking you when you remove its grip. Insecurity only has power over you when you allow it control over your thoughts."

FIXED MIND-SETS AND GROWTH MIND-SETS

A friend left this thought on my Facebook page: "We do what we do and feel how we feel because we think what we think."[2] And you know what pattern of thought feeds our insecurities most? A fixed mind-set versus a growth mind-set.

People with fixed mind-sets see their abilities, talents, skills, relationships, and intelligence as limited and lacking. Where they are today is where they will always be. Things can't get better. It is what it is. Applying this Best Yes wisdom isn't really possible for people like me.

People with growth mind-sets see their abilities, talents, skills, relationships, and intelligence with potential. Where they are today is a starting place, not a finish line. Things can get better. They can grow and develop and persevere to get to improved places. Using wisdom to make Best Yes decisions is possible!

Mind-set is a simple idea discovered by world-renowned Stanford University psychologist Carol Dweck in decades of research. She says:

> In a fixed mindset, people believe their basic qualities, like their intelligence or talent, are simply fixed traits. They

spend their time documenting their intelligence or talent instead of developing them. They also believe that talent alone creates success—without effort. They're wrong.

In a growth mindset, people believe that their most basic abilities can be developed through dedication and hard work—brains and talent are just the starting point. This view creates a love of learning and a resilience that is essential for great accomplishment.[3]

I am fascinated by this research by Dweck because it lines up so beautifully with what the Bible says about how to grow past our insecurities. We don't have to just manage our insecurities, deal with our insecurities, or grit our teeth and will ourselves to somehow ignore them. We can grow past them.

We find security when we tie our mind-sets to the potential of Jesus' work in us. Indeed, we are limited in and of ourselves. But the minute we receive Jesus to be the Lord of our lives, our limited potential can turn into exponential growth. He is alive in us. He gives us freedom from our dead lives and the power to walk in a new life—a resurrected life. Romans 8:10–16 says,

> When God lives and breathes in you (and he does, as surely as he did in Jesus), you are delivered from that dead life. With his Spirit living in you, your body will be as alive as Christ's! So don't you see that we don't owe this old do-it-yourself life one red cent. There's nothing in it for us, nothing at all. The best thing to do is give it a decent burial and get on with your new life. God's Spirit beckons. There are things to do and places to go! This resurrection life you received from God is not a timid, grave-tending life.

It's adventurously expectant, greeting God with a child-like "What's next, Papa?" (MSG)

I love those words, "God's Spirit beckons." Yes. Yes, He does. I was reading this section to a friend who told me she doesn't really feel insecure, but when I read her that sentence, "God's Spirit beckons," she sighed. And then admitted, "I know that feeling. God beckoning. And maybe that's the reason I don't get insecure. For years I've refused to step away from what is comfortable to me. I've refused to step into anything that I'm not sure I can do. So, I don't often feel insecure because I stay in only secure places and refuse God beckoning me to more."

Yes, I love that God is beckoning all of us, beckoning us to a Best Yes. Or maybe many Best Yes opportunities. Whether we feel insecure and limited—or we feel secure because we intentionally limit ourselves by staying in only those places where we feel naturally secure—either way, we are stunting possible growth.

We can't grow when insecurities keep us from the life-giving oxygen of transformational truth. God beckons or invites me to change my mind-set from focusing on my insecurities and limitations to His security and limitless potential.

I have to change from a fixed mind-set to a growth mind-set.

"The fixed mindset," Dweck says, "creates an internal mono-logue that is focused on judging: 'This means I'm a loser' . . . 'This means I'm a bad husband.'"[4] In other words, I chain my identity to my insecurity. My identity is that I'm a child of God just as those verses from Romans 8 state. But I take my circum-stances, the opinions of others, and my own skewed feelings and chain them to my identity link by link. Then I say:

I am a child of God, *but* look at what a mess my finances
are.

I am a child of God, *but* I'm fifty pounds overweight and
feel like such a failure.

I am a child of God, *but* look what choice my kid just
made that makes our family look bad.

Then I allow my insecurity to be the first thing that walks
into every decision I make. Therefore, I stay in the fixed mind-
set that progress isn't possible for a person like me or a family
like mine.

CUT THE BUT!

On the other hand, when I change to a growth mind-set, I
don't chain my identity to my insecurity. Instead, I chain my
identity to the Word of God that breathes hope and powerful
potential back into any situation.

Every time I say I am a child of God, I have to remove the
but and instead use the word *therefore* to usher God's promise
into my reality. We must cut the *but*!

I am a child of God, *therefore* I don't have to be afraid or
dismayed. I know God is with me. He will strengthen
me, help me, and uphold me with His hand (Isa. 41:10).

I am a child of God, *therefore* no weapon formed against
me shall succeed. God will disprove every tongue that
rises against me in judgment (Isa. 54:17 ESV).

I am a child of God, *therefore* God is in my midst, a

mighty one who will save me; He will rejoice over me
with gladness; He will quiet me with his love; He will
exult over me with loud singing (Zeph. 3:17).
I am a child of God, *therefore* God's Word is there for
me. It is a lamp to my feet and a light to my path (Ps.
119:105).

In 2 Timothy 2:9, Paul reminded us that though we can be
chained as he was as a prisoner, "God's word is not chained."
There is a double meaning here. God's Word is at work in the
world even without our involvement. Despite Paul being in
prison, the gospel continued to spread. But we can also see that
even when we are in chains, God's Word is still at work within
us. In other words, when we tie our identities to God's truth,
God's Word can and will lift us above the insecurities holding
us down, taking us under, and threatening to drown us.

All this sounds good in theory, but does it really work?
It does. One of the places I can feel as if I'm drowning in insecurity is in my marriage. I love my man. He loves me. I know
he loves me with every fiber of my being except this one place
in my heart that trips me up sometimes. This place where a
wound exists.

Early in our marriage, Art admitted to me he wished I'd
lose weight. Please don't judge this precious man of mine. He
was young and naïve about what this would do to my heart. I
had gained a lot of weight with my first pregnancy and then
got pregnant again quickly with our second child. I was feeling insecure and was trying to get him to reassure me with
lots of leading questions. But in a moment of honesty, he did
the exact opposite.

It ripped something wide open in my heart, and a flood of insecurities rushed in quickly and I felt like I was nine again. In that pool. Going under. Disoriented. Cut off from the oxygen I knew I needed but couldn't figure out how to get.

I spent weeks planning how I could leave him. I wanted out. It wasn't just what he said. It's what I did with what he said. I took what he said and played it all the way out in the most negative way I could. In my brain, his small admission that he wished I'd lose weight suddenly became: *He doesn't find me attractive. He'll probably start being attracted to other women. So he'll probably have an affair. He'll probably leave me in a wake of rejection and shame. To avoid all the awful pain, I'd better leave him now.*

I had a fixed mind-set that his one comment would forever limit and eventually kill our marriage. I was a child of God, *but* since my daddy had left me early in life, it shouldn't surprise me my husband would eventually do the exact same thing.

Insecurity gripped me so tightly, truth couldn't get in— until Art looked at me lost in my own horrible thoughts one night and said, "You know we should call our fights growth opportunities, right? Because that's what they are. Signs that we're growing. And as long as our relationship is growing, it's living. I'm so sorry I hurt you. I love you, Lysa. I want to grow through this with you."

I had a choice right then and there. I could have the fixed mind-set that we didn't have what it would take to persevere and therefore strip the hope right out of our marriage. A hopeless marriage quickly becomes a dead marriage. Or I could have a growth mind-set that even though I didn't feel good about things today, that didn't mean things couldn't get good.

We could grow, both of us, together. We are children of God, *therefore* all things are possible—even a marriage that isn't always easy.

And so we stayed. I'm convinced that a growth mind-set has saved my marriage many times over. We still have lots of growth opportunities. In fact, we had one this past week when I got so mad I thought my eyeballs were going to pop right out of my head! And I may or may not have called him a name, one that you can actually find in the Bible that starts with an *A* and ends in an *S*. Three letters. Only I didn't mean it in the biblical sense. If you know what I mean. But I'm crazy about my man. I really am.

I don't know what kind of decision you have to make today. But I write all this to issue a challenge for this chapter: we must let our identity, not our insecurity, be the first thing that walks into every situation we face—every decision we make.

We must let our identity, not our insecurity, be the first thing that walks into every situation we face—every decision we make.

If we are going to live in the thrilling place of Best Yes opportunities, we must cut the *but* of lies chaining us to insecurities. Then and only then can we stop choking from the lack of truth.

This really is a "we" thing. So many of us deal with this. Today I tweeted and Facebooked the following: "Insecurity. I'm writing about this today and would love your thoughts." Almost instantaneously I received a flood of responses from different women in different places, stages, and scenarios: a single ER doctor in Chicago, a missionary in Africa, a young mom headed to a playgroup and dreading feeling less than the other moms. The first response said,

> @LysaTerKeurst 140 characters isn't nearly enough to share all the thoughts on insecurity. so. many.

Just as our bodies need oxygen, our souls need truth flowing steadily in and out. I don't remember how I was saved at the pool that day. But I know how awful it was to get so disoriented that I didn't know where safety was. So, for you who are there, I want to weave myself into your story. I'm standing in the shallow end. I'm holding tightly on to an immovable bar of truth with one hand—and with the other, I'm reaching toward you.

Just as our bodies need oxygen, our souls need truth flowing steadily in and out.

Grab hold. Come back from the sinking place. And from the deepest place of your soul, catch your breath.

Chapter 17

The Very Best Yes

FOR ALL SEVENTEEN YEARS OF HER LIFE, THIS GIRL, MY middle girl, has known a secret. When it all falls apart, there is a safe place. Her mom's arms. More than a hug, this place beats with the gentle rhythm of a heart that feels what she feels. So my girl brings what she can't bear to experience alone into this place. And we reconnect.

The cord that was cut all those years ago in the delivery room forced her to live and breathe on her own. But while it separated our bodies, nothing can sever our hearts. What she feels, I still very much feel.

Joy by joy. Pain by pain. Thrill by thrill. Tear by tear. Celebration by celebration. Disappointment by disappointment. She feels it. I feel it.

And it's not just because I gave birth to her. No, I have adopted kids too. And this unseen cord of connection is the same. Even if you don't have children, I suspect you still know these feelings of deep love and care that can tether one soul to another.

This instinct of knowing, feeling, stirring, wrestling, and pulsing is an unusual sense of understanding. What touches someone I love touches me.

So, when my daughter crawled into my arms at the 3:00 a.m. hour a few nights ago, I knew. Trouble had found its way into her heart. A boy, whom she thought would handle her heart gently, didn't. Her crush, crushed her.

HUNGRY, ANGRY, LONELY, TIRED

This time right now is hard. This hard time is strewn with pieces of a broken heart not able to be held together and soothed with the princess Band-Aids of a few years ago. This isn't the time for this sweet girl to make decisions on her own.

Her tears cloud her Best Yes vision. Her loneliness causes her heart to feel a bit weak right now. Sleep sometimes escapes her. Dreams sometimes betray her. And waking up some days with that same throbbing hurt is like a rug being ripped out from under her all over again.

I realize it's a simple teenage heartbreak. I know that in a few years it will be but a silly memory she rolls her eyes at, thanking the good Lord above for allowing this breakup to happen. I can see all that. But for now, in the middle of it all, she can't.

Plus, social media magnifies it all: his disinterest in her; his new interest in other girls; his quandary of who to take to the prom; his candlelit ask of another girl. All within one week, all this and more was posted for all the world to see. It's hard.

She feels it all so deeply. And while I can see it's all for the best, I hurt for this girl with a split-open heart because she's mine—my girl who couldn't sleep so she slipped into my bed to be near the rhythmic heartbeat she's known since she was conceived.

And in the quiet middle of the night, I hold her. I brush her long brown hair off her tear-streaked face. I kiss the wet salt on her cheeks. And I whisper, "I love you."

And she knows I'm safe. Her safe place to run and find when the world gets wild and cruel and heartbreakingly mean.

The next morning she shows me the source of her middle-of-the-night anguish, a text message from him. His words were from a heart entangled with immaturity and his own sources of hurt. He's not a bad person. He's young. And sometimes young means incapable of handling situations the right way.

I understand that. Age has given me that gift. But my young girl did not understand. She took the words like daggers to the heart. And cried.

She handed me the phone.

"Help me reply."

There we sat in the midst of poached eggs and toast crumbs talking together, thinking together, replying together.

Together is a really good word. Together is what we need when we hit tough patches in life. Making decisions when life is making you cry shouldn't be done alone.

No matter what hard place we find ourselves in, feeling alone can make us vulnerable to bad decisions. In several recovery programs, they teach people trying to break addictions to

"Together" is a really good word. Together is what we need when we hit tough patches in life. Making decisions when life is making you cry shouldn't be done alone.

HALT before making a decision in a hard place. When you are *hungry, angry, lonely,* or *tired,* you can get quite vulnerable. Part of recovery is learning to pay attention to these inner signals and use appropriate ways of getting needs met that stay in line with sobriety. I like that.

And I think it can be useful for even those not in recovery programs. Hard places can so easily make us want to default to using our feelings rather than wisdom as our guide. That's not the best time to make a decision. At least not alone.

In those moments when we feel swept away in a current of fast-moving feelings, we need to pause. Wait. Let someone else be there as a voice of clarity.

I suspect if you're in a tough place, it probably feels more significant than a teenaged heartbreak. I understand. I've been there. And I'll probably be there again. And when we're there, we have to be honest that we're not in the place to make big decisions right then. Maybe we're not even in the place to make decisions on simple requests by others.

This doesn't make you bad or incapable. It makes you smart. Smart enough to know to pause and take extra time when life takes on extenuating circumstances that are hard.

In this pause from decisions, go to your safe place. When the world beats you down, open up your Bible. Let His sentences finish yours. Let truth walk before you like a guide on a dark path.

And go also to someone in your sphere of influence whom you know is wise. Let them help you. Stand on top of their wisdom when you feel shaky with your own. Gaining a new altitude can recalibrate our attitudes. When we can rise up on the wisdom of others and get a new view of our situations, our next steps seem a little clearer.

How do we know whom to go to? The Bible makes it clear:

> Who is wise and understanding among you? Let them show it by their good life, by deeds done in the humility that comes from wisdom. But if you harbor bitter envy and selfish ambition in your hearts, do not boast about it or deny the truth. Such "wisdom" does not come down from heaven but is earthly, unspiritual, demonic. For where you have envy and selfish ambition, there you find disorder and every evil practice.
>
> But the wisdom that comes from heaven is first of all pure; then peace-loving, considerate, submissive, full of mercy and good fruit, impartial and sincere. (James 3:13–17)

There's a whole lot of good text here. But I want to focus on one phrase that really helps me know who has the kind of wisdom I want to turn to when I feel too uncertain to make decisions on my own—"the humility that comes from wisdom."

Humility and wisdom are a package deal. And often the people who have the most wisdom have experienced the most humility. Or sometimes even the most humiliation. A wisdom like none other can arise from those hard places that bring us low.

When I'm going through stuff that makes it hard to make good decisions, I want to turn to people who have been through some stuff. And not just people who went through hard times, but those who came out on the other side carrying some wisdom from which I can learn. Real wisdom—wisdom that's been unearthed in the messy, untidy, mud-puddle places of life. When this kind of wisdom sits in the heart of a person who is vulnerable enough to drop their pride and share what they know—that's a gift, a gift I desperately need when going through some stuff.

I STOOD ON HER WISDOM

Just a few weeks ago I was in that place of needing someone who has some of that hard-earned wisdom. I had a major decision to make in the midst of getting some really hard news. One of my college-aged kids had done something that completely stunned me. And I was two days from leaving to speak at one of the biggest events of my life when I found out.

My first instinct was to cancel the trip. I curled up in my bed and cried. I could literally feel my heart drumming against the mattress with such force I started to worry I might be having a heart attack. I called my doctor and asked if someone could check my blood pressure. They wound up giving me an EKG and telling me I have the heart of a very healthy athlete. I guess EKGs can't detect the kind of brokenness my heart was experiencing.

I finally mustered up the energy to open my computer and figure out how to word my cancellation e-mail. I had never canceled an event before, so I whispered a prayer asking God to please confirm He was okay with me canceling.

That's when I saw an e-mail from my assistant telling me another speaker had canceled from this event and they were requesting I do two keynote messages. *Are you kidding me? I'm thinking I will not even be able to deliver one message, much less two!*

I knew I needed to stand on the wisdom from someone else who'd gone before me. Someone who had been through some stuff with her kids and still had to find the courage to speak.

So I called another speaker I knew had some wisdom found in those places of humility and humiliation. It wasn't an easy to call to make. I cringed at how raw and exposed this admission made me feel. It's much easier to paint on a smile and pretend. But I knew I was safe with her because we'd had a conversation years ago where she shared some of the less-than-perfect dynamics in her family.

I called. And her words were a gift.

She was generous with her transparency. She assured me I wasn't alone with words like, "Me too," "I know," "We are going through our own hurts and disappointments even right now." There was not a drop of disgrace directed toward me in her voice. It was interesting I'd read Proverbs 11:2 just that morning: "When pride comes, then comes disgrace, but with humility comes wisdom."

Yes, I knew from where her wisdom came.

And then she settled my wildly beating heart: "You're not alone, Lysa. The grace our audiences need is the same grace we must walk in daily. Let this hurt work for you, not against you. Go. You must go."

I knew she was right. Wise. I stood on her wisdom and replied I would do both keynotes. After deciding to go to the conference, I called and informed my adult child that we were going to do this trip together.

We flew to the event together. We walked through the hard place together. And in the midst of being humbled to the point of humiliation, I discovered my own hard-earned wisdom.

I wouldn't have made that decision on my own. My feelings were begging me to cancel. But my friend's wisdom lifted me above my feelings. And as I stood in the midst of her wisdom bossing my feelings, I discovered my Best Yes for this conference.

I'm not saying that you should never cancel. Nor am I saying we should take canceling lightly. We shouldn't. Don't miss the real point here. The point is how crucial it is to seek out wise counsel when we feel a bit swallowed up by circumstances and situations.

Also, please note I didn't call my friends whom I knew would simply agree with me that canceling was a good idea. I called this friend whom I knew had wisdom. And though I had no idea what advice she would give, I knew it would come from a place of experience, honesty, humility, and, yes, wisdom. And in listening to her, I opened the door to gaining my own wisdom in the midst of this heartbreak.

AND THEN I FOUND THE SILVER LINING

You know, some moments of life are amazing. Beyond amazing. Blessed treasures.

Then there are other moments, the ones not often discussed, the ones when we feel like a complete failure. Those are the moments that taste bitter, like this situation with my adult child, not sweet, the ones that won't make it into the family scrapbook. We wonder if we really have what it takes to do the assignments placed before us. Yes, those kinds of unglued heart moments aren't the ones we capture in pictures. But there is a silver lining I've discovered in those moments: a compassionate kind of wisdom I can't get any other way.

Wisdom is our silver lining. Wisdom will help us not repeat the mistakes we've made but rather grow stronger through them.

How do we find it? We come to the Lord and ask Him for it. We set aside our excuses, our habits, and our justifications and whisper, "I need Your perspective, God. I come before You and humbly admit my desperate dependence on You." As Proverbs 11:2 reminded us, "with humility comes wisdom."

Yes, humility.

But wisdom can come from those times of humiliation as well.

Remember King David? He had an affair with a married woman named Bathsheba. When Bathsheba sent word to David she was pregnant with his baby, he panicked and had her husband killed so he could quickly marry her.

Sin and consequences always walk hand in hand.

His choice brought calamity upon his house, and the son born to him and Bathsheba died. Sin and consequences always walk hand in hand. And David surely suffered the consequences of his choices for years to come.

But mixed in with the heartbreak and the humiliation, something else happened. When the repentant David went to comfort Bathsheba, she became pregnant with Solomon. From this relationship wrapped in humiliation came the man the Bible describes this way:

> God gave Solomon wisdom and very great insight, and a breadth of understanding as measureless as the sand on the seashore. Solomon's wisdom was greater than the wisdom of all the people of the East, and greater than all the wisdom of Egypt. He was wiser than anyone else, including Ethan the Ezrahite—wiser than Heman, Kalkol and Darda, the sons of Mahol. And his fame spread to all the surrounding nations. He spoke three thousand proverbs and his songs numbered a thousand and five. He spoke about plant life, from the cedar of Lebanon to the hyssop that grows out of walls. He also spoke about animals and birds, reptiles and fish. From all nations people came to listen to Solomon's wisdom, sent by all the kings of the world, who had heard of his wisdom. (1 Kings 4:29–34)

From humiliation great wisdom came.

Humility and humiliation, silver linings that can lead to wisdom.

WISDOM AND JOY FOUND IN THE STRANGEST PLACES

Only now can I start to understand what James was talking about when he instructs us to "consider it pure joy, my brothers and sisters, whenever you face trials of many kinds" (1:2). Doesn't that sound like a contradictory statement? Joy from trials? Yes, at first it seems quite strange. Until we realize he's telling us to "consider it pure joy." In other words, through a lens of wisdom, look for joy in this unlikely place of trial. And then Scripture tells us something else in the next couple of verses. Something quite confirming in light of all we've been talking about:

> Because you know that the testing of your faith produces perseverance. Let perseverance finish its work so that you may be mature and complete, not lacking anything. If any of you lacks wisdom, you should ask God, who gives generously to all without finding fault, and it will be given to you. But when you ask, you must believe and not doubt, because the one who doubts is like a wave of the sea, blown and tossed by the wind. That person should not expect to receive anything from the Lord. Such a person is double-minded and unstable in all they do. Believers in humble circumstances ought to take pride in their high position. (vv. 3–9)

Trials are working something good in us we can't get any other way. We can find joy in that.

If we persevere, we will become mature, complete, and not lacking anything. We can find joy in that.

If we lack wisdom, we should ask God and He'll give it to us as long as we don't doubt. We can find joy in that.

Believers who are in humble circumstances are in a high position. We can find joy in that.

So, yes, I can now consider all this and find pure joy when I face trials. And I can gain wisdom in the midst of it all—wisdom I need, wisdom I can use to make even better decisions in the future, and wisdom others will need that I now have to give.

Just as my seventeen-year-old daughter knew where to go with her broken heart, I know where to go with mine, because even wisdom-hunters feel tired and sad sometimes. Even when we're considering the joy, we can still feel hurt so deeply. And while God can see it's all for the best, I know He still hurts when I'm just a girl with a split-open heart. Because I'm His— His girl who couldn't sleep, so as my tears slipped, I opened up His Word to be near the rhythm of His heartbeat. In the quiet middle of my pain, He held me.

I know I'm safe. He is our safe place to run when the world gets wild and cruel and heartbreakingly mean. And God whispers, "I love you. This time spent searching for Me and My truths? This desperate dependence on Me? This is your very Best Yes."

Chapter 18

When My Best Yes Doesn't Yield What I Expect

I STOOD AT THE VENDING MACHINE INFURIATED. MORE than annoyed. More than mad. More than angry. Infuriated.

A girl can sometimes have responses out of proportion to the wrong she is experiencing. And like a compass pointing to true north, this infuriation pointed somewhere I didn't want to explore.

I wanted a Diet Coke. So I did what was required. I followed the rules. I put in the required money. I pushed the right button. Only what I got wasn't at all what I wanted. Something had gone wrong.

I clenched my fists and bit my lip. And I knew. My out-of-proportion response wasn't really about a soda. It was about being disillusioned—by one of my teens. It was about my feeling that if I did all the right things, I would get all the right results. You do what's expected of you and you'll get what you expect: put in the money, push the button, get the Diet Coke.

Put in all the time—love, daddy-daughter date nights, intentionality, prayer, discipline, Bible lessons, Sundays at church, dinners at the table, talks at bedtime, kisses, hugs, and chores.

Push the button.

Get the child who walks the straight and narrow. But no. Sometimes you get the unexpected.

And you know what I'm tempted to do as a mom? Draw a straight line from my child's wrong choice to my weakness in mothering. That will just about kill a mama. Crack her heart open and fill it with paralyzing regret of the past and fear for the future. And that's exactly where Satan wants us mamas to stay. Paralyzed.

But what if that's the wrong line to draw? What if I'm supposed to draw a straight line from my child's wrong choice to my *strength* in mothering?

What if God said, "What mama is strong enough, persevering enough, tough enough to bend without breaking under the weight of the choices this child will make? What mama is willing to be humbled to the point of humiliation, yet not blinded to the wisdom found like diamonds in dirty places? What mama will not just pray about this child but will truly pray this child all the way through their stuff? What mama will be courageous enough to let Me write her child's story?"

And then God points. I can't say I ever wanted God to be pointing in my direction. I can't. But sometimes we get the unexpected.

We make the best decision we know to make. We pray. We ask God to guide us. We walk with Him and talk with Him and trust Him. We read the Christian books and get the Christian advice. We hang with Christians and sing the praise songs and use words like *blessed, calling,* and *fellowship.* We gather around the potluck dinner and wonder why the worship leader looks cool in an outfit that would look ridiculous on us.

We do all that. And still.

The unexpected barges in and announces he's staying for a while. Like a cuss word yelled by a heckler in a church service, it catches us off guard, makes us squirm, and needs to be ushered out of the building. But it lingers. And people whisper about it. And we wonder if the pastor should keep on preaching or call it a day.

Cuss words aren't supposed to be heard in church. And good mamas aren't supposed to feel like failures.

And wives who have loved well aren't supposed to be told their husbands have had affairs or find their husbands are addicted to porn.

And men who have worked hard, stayed late, and given all their best to a boss who treats them poorly aren't supposed to be fired.

And adopted parents aren't supposed to have to give the answer to a million prayers back to a biological mom who will get high this afternoon.

And professional women aren't supposed to be told they can't have the big accounts because they refuse to go to the strip clubs with seedy clients.

And cancellation notices aren't supposed to be sent from a would-be bride flushed red with rejection.

You know what I'm saying? Have you ever felt knocked off-kilter by the unexpected?

And then suddenly a well-meaning friend drives up in her clean minivan, sporting a bumper sticker that says, "My child memorized the entire gospel of John at VBS last week—nanny, nanny, boo boo, stick your head in doo doo." Her husband has the dream job with a dream income. Her fallopian tubes work. Her legs are thin and her skin is clear and she hands me a card with Habakkuk 3:17–18 hand-calligraphed on the front:

> Though the fig tree does not bud and there are no grapes on the vines, though the olive crop fails and the fields produce no food, though there are no sheep in the pen and no cattle in the stalls, yet I will rejoice in the LORD, I will be joyful in God my Savior.

Awesome verse. Terrible timing. I just want to tell her to go stick her figs, olives, grapes, sheep, and cattle where the sun don't shine.

I wonder if Mary, the mother of Jesus, ever felt this way. God told her she was blessed and highly favored. Then unexpectedly screamed a cuss word in her church. Her groom doubted her. The whispers of others surely stung. She gave birth in a barn. With no clean sheets, trained doctor, or epidural, I might add.

Then she became a woman on the run like a wanted criminal while evil hunted down her child with a dagger in its hand and blood crusted on its fingers.

She escaped death's hunt for her child then but not forever. Most devastating of all, she collapsed in the shadow of a cross while the body of the boy she birthed hung with the life draining slowly and pooling in a puddle of shame at her feet. All she could recognize about Him was His voice gurgling the last words through gasps for air.

If that's what highly favored is, my God, let me stand in another line. If that's where Best Yes decisions sometimes lead, then let's change the radio dial to a completely different station. But that's when we have to make an intentional shift. We must draw different lines to different conclusions.

Often when things don't add up, we throw a spotlight on our weaknesses, don't we?

This situation stinks because I stink as a person.

My child failed because I failed as a mother.

My ministry didn't take off like I expected it to because I'm not smart enough, or schooled enough, or business minded enough.

I try so hard. I give it all I've got. Then it all just falls apart. And it all just seems incredibly out of whack.

Let this unexpected happening point to your strength, not your weakness. Maybe you've been entrusted with this. Not cursed with it.

But don't you see, in the midst of the unexpected, we have the opportunity to make one of our greatest Best Yes decisions ever? Let this unexpected happening point to your strength, not your weakness. Maybe you've been entrusted with this. Not cursed with it.

DO THE NEXT RIGHT THING THAT'S RIGHT IN FRONT OF YOU

My pastor preached a sermon yesterday about why Jesus waited four days and for the death of Lazarus before He answered Mary and Martha's urgent cry for Him to come. Four days! Four days! By then Lazarus was dead, wrapped in grave cloths, and buried behind a stone. And Jesus did this to people He loved dearly.

Why? With a tenderness that shook the hearts of all there, my pastor said, "Jesus had already shown the world He could heal. Now He needed to show all that He could resurrect. They had to know that."

We all stood to our feet and clapped. Not for our pastor. We clapped because truth settled into deep places that needed a personal resurrection. Some unexpected hurts require more than just healing. Paralyzed places that feel dead inside us need a full-on resurrection.

In the short term, this will make no sense. It will hurt. It will cause tears to fall and anger so fierce to rise, you didn't even know you were capable of such feelings. But don't get paralyzed. Do the next right thing that's right in front of you. And then do the next right thing. Take baby steps of right decisions, and soon you will walk with a new strength you never knew was possible.

Good mamas who feel like failures, do the next right thing right in front of you. Call a friend, a friend who has tasted hard stuff with her own kids. Talk. Glean. Pray together. Go tell your children their mistakes don't define them. Or you. And mean it.

Do the next right thing that's right in front of you.

Wives who have loved well but haven't been loved well, do the next right thing right in front of you. Write down promises from God's Word. Every time those voices of hurt and betrayal haunt you, speak truth louder. Scream it if you have to. And find a Christian counselor to speak truth right alongside you.

Men who have worked hard but have been fired in the face of unfairness, do the next right thing right in front of you. Make a list of your transferrable skills—those qualities that made you amazing at the tasks you carried out. Ask God to direct you to ways to provide for your family in the short term and long term.

No matter what wrong thing has happened, there is a right next thing to do.

"In any moment of decision, the best thing you can do is the right thing. The worst thing you can do is nothing." That's from Theodore Roosevelt, and though I don't consider him a brilliant theologian, he was a man who could have easily been paralyzed when the unexpected came barging in.

From that cracked-open-heart place, a God-breathed strength will rise. Rise. Rise. And help you spit in Satan's face as you declare, "You picked the wrong woman to mess with this time!"

His young bride died after giving birth to their daughter. That would have been horrible enough. But the unexpected hit Roosevelt with a double dose of grief that day because just hours earlier, in the same house, his mother had died of typhoid fever. Historians say he wrote a large X on the page of his diary that February 14, 1884, and then, "The light has gone out of my life."[1]

That kind of unexpected could surely have paralyzed a man. Maybe it did for a season. But I also know from the history books he came back. And it appears there was a strength that the unexpected had not snuffed out. Maybe, just maybe, the unexpected actually served to bring his strength to the place it matched his eventual assignment. For just twelve years later, in 1898, he was elected governor, in 1900 vice president, and then upon McKinley's assassination in 1901, at forty-two years old he became the youngest president of the United States.[2]

Friend, you are strong. You are persevering, tough, able to bend without breaking, willing to be humbled to the point of humiliation, not blinded, a hunter for wisdom, a praying-through-it woman, a courageous gal, one who wants to learn the deep dependence of following hard after God Himself.

Let me reach through these fragile, typed-out letters and take your hand. And stand with you. From that cracked-open-heart place, a God-breathed strength will rise. Rise. Rise. And help you spit in Satan's face as you declare, "You picked the wrong woman to mess with this time!"

(And, by golly, if you see a woman like this, hand her a real Diet Coke. She probably needs a little liquid heaven right about now.)

Chapter 19

We Make Choices. Then Our Choices Make Us.

I'M NOT MUCH OF A BAKER. THOUGH I HAVE MOST OF THE stuff a baker would need. If someone didn't know me and piddled about in my kitchen, they might think I'm of the baking kind. "She's got an apron, pans, measuring cups, vanilla, sugar, flour, and recipe books. Maybe she's a baker."

But should they lean in a little closer to examine my pans, they'd see they are too clean. Too shiny. Too new and unused looking.

No, she's not a baker. She's a woman who occasionally gets a wild baking hair. But for the most part she's thankful for the grocery-store bakers who whip up nice things she can bring home and repackage into her Tupperware carrier. It's not that she's trying to be deceptive with the baked goods—just slightly creative. She can't help the assumptions people make when she puts something into a Tupperware cake carrier.

Ahem.

Anyhow, I won't be featured on any sort of Food Network baking show. Or even asked to contribute to the school bake sale. Because maybe the real baking moms (whom I admire with all my heart plus a cherry on the top) might have figured out my little grocery-store trick and stopped asking.

So a baker I am not. But I love the thought of it. I love the thought of pulling out things that don't normally go together and plopping them in a bowl just because the recipe said so. Like eggs with flour. Vanilla with sugar. Baking soda and milk.

If I sat down to eat these unlikely pairs just by themselves, I'd be sadly disappointed. But mix them all together using just the right recipe, and they make delicious things. Really delicious things that I want to eat and share with others. With moderation of course, my fellow *Made to Crave* friends.

But imagine if I plopped all the ingredients of this amazing cake recipe into a bowl but refused to stir it. There would be shiny yellow yolks on top of crisp white flour with a dab or two of brown from the vanilla. Little mounds of sugar would sit off to the side of the bowl along with the baking soda. The milk splashed on top would sink into the flour bottom. I would have a bowl full of potential that will never be if I don't stir before baking. I'm not exactly sure what might happen if I just dumped this all into a pan and popped it into the oven, unstirred, but I know it wouldn't come out right.

That's the way it is with all the wisdom ingredients we've been talking about throughout this book. They aren't meant to be examined individually.

They are meant to be stirred together as they stir your heart. Individually, all we've talked about are pinches of experience, dashes of insight, spoonfuls of inspiration, and cups of truth; but stir them together and they form a mixture of maturity. And the person who then lets maturity bake in the heat of everyday life will persevere in pleasing God. As Eugene Peterson says, we must desire to "have long obedience in the same direction." Choice by choice. Day by day. We must stir into our lives all we've learned.

"Let perseverance finish its work so that you may be mature and complete, not lacking anything. If any of you lacks wisdom, you should ask God, who gives generously to all without finding fault, and it will be given to you" (James 1:4–5).

Over time you will gain a heart of wisdom. And from your heart of wisdom, all your Best Yes answers will come.

It's not the activities or accomplishments we string together that make lives well lived as much as it is the hearts of wisdom we gain and use along the way.

And I'm convinced more and more of something regarding a heart of wisdom. It's not the activities or accomplishments we string together that make lives well lived as much as it is the hearts of wisdom we gain and use along the way.

Every day we make choices. Then our choices make us. We have options. We make choices. Then we live the lingering effects, good and bad, of those decisions. And those decisions determine so much about our lives. Much of what I live today is the result of the choices I made yesterday.

Understanding this helps me feel the weight of the decisions I will make today. What a glorious or ominous thing this might be for me. Oh, that I might stir into my life a well-done heart of wisdom.

WE EACH HAVE A PART TO PLAY

C. S. Lewis wrote:

> Every time you make a choice you are turning the central part of you, the part of you that chooses, into something a little different than it was before.
>
> And taking your life as a whole, with all your innumerable choices, all your life long you are slowly turning this central thing into a heavenly creature or a hellish creature: either into a creature that is in harmony with God, and with other creatures, and with itself, or else into one that is in a state of war and hatred with God, and with its fellow creatures, and with itself.
>
> To be the one kind of creature is heaven: that is, it is joy and peace and knowledge and power. To be the other means madness, horror, idiocy, rage, impotence,

and eternal loneliness. Each of us at each moment is progressing to the one state or the other.[1]

Oh, God, might I be turning that central part of me, the part that chooses, into something different than it was before. Might I be stirring into that part of me all the ingredients of maturity and wisdom and perseverance. Yes, I want to be more than I was before. More because I read the pages of this book, yes. But even more because the pages of Scriptures woven throughout this message folded themselves into the mixture of my heart.

There is a subtle space in which I let my mind be completely truthful about what's really going on. It's often a brief few moments in between the rush of responsibilities when I exhale and unfiltered honesty rushes in.

Descriptions ping in my head. But this time they are different. Instead of being the woman who is overwhelmed with my schedule, aching with the sadness of an underwhelmed soul, I'm changing—slowly. I'm using the power of the small no—mostly. And I'm chasing down my decisions, considering the trade, and showing up for practice. I'm searching for the unrushed Best Yes decisions.

I don't do it all perfectly. But I absolutely look for more and more moments of the unbroken companionship with the Giver of all wisdom.

Yes, I'm changing.

And I pray you are too.

Wisdom is either displayed or betrayed by our actions. As Jesus said, "Wisdom is proved right by her deeds" (Matt. 11:19). So let's choose wisdom. Let's use the two most powerful words, *yes* and *no*, with resounding assurance, graceful clarity, and guided power. All so people may see Jesus when they see us. Hear Jesus when they hear us. And know Jesus when they know us.

Indeed, in God's plan, you and I have a part to play. If we know it and believe it, we'll live it. We'll live our lives making decisions with the Best Yes as our best filter. We'll be a grand display of God's Word lived out. Our undistracted love will make our faith ring true. Our wisdom will help us make decisions that will still be good tomorrow. And we'll be alive and present for all of it.

Now let's go and live the Best Yes life.

The Lord makes firm the steps of the one who delights in him; though he may stumble, he will not fall, for the Lord upholds him with his hand.

—PSALM 37:23–24

Acknowledgments

THIS BOOK STARTED WITH A THOUGHT. THE THOUGHT WAS how the very simple words of *yes* and *no* really are two of the most powerful words. How we use those two words determines so much about how we live our lives . . . how we spend our souls. So I dared to whisper these thoughts into the hearts closest to me, just to see, would it resonate with them? Their nods of approval turned into thousands of words that would be talked about, written, edited, rewritten, and discussed in countless meetings and phone calls. My simple thoughts, words, and stories were gently guided along by the many people with whom I have the honor of doing life and ministry. In various ways, their fingerprints dance all inside this book. I thank God for weaving these lives into mine.

> Art . . . I love you. I love doing life with you. And I love that you let me be me.
> Jackson, Mark, Hope, Ashley, and Brooke . . . my priority blessings whom I love so very much.

Paige, Philecia, Kenzie, Madalyn, Megan W., Meghan Y.
...my added blessings whom I love as if you were my
own.

Meredith...you are truly amazing and gifted beyond
measure.

Leah, Lindsay, Laurie...I couldn't do this without your
love, laughter, and talents.

Barb, Lisa A., Glynnis, Amy, Renee, Karen, Melissa, Teri,
Alison, Kaley, and all the Proverbs 31 Ministries gals...
the best team.

The P31 Board...the smartest people I know.

Christine, Sheila, Patsy, Lisa, Liz, Angela...treasured
friends.

Pastor and my family at Elevation...doing life with you
is a gift.

Lisa C. and Kristi...angels with skin on.

The "In the Loop" Group...you make ministry so very
fun and meaningful.

Esther, Brian, Joel, Chad, Katy, Emily, Janene, Lori,
Belinda...you know books better than anyone and it's
one of my greatest joys to work with you all.

Robin, Christine, John, TJ, Greg, and the C2 crew...you
know how to bring the group lessons to life in beautiful
ways.

Things I Don't Want You to Forget

CHAPTER 1: CHECK THE THIRD BOX

We must not confuse the command to *love* with the disease to *please*.

In God's plan, you've got a *part to play*. If you know it and believe it, you'll live it.

CHAPTER 2: THE WAY OF THE BEST YES

If we want His direction for our decisions, the great *cravings* of our *souls* must not only be the big moments of assignment. They must also be the seemingly small instructions in the most ordinary of moments when God points His Spirit finger, saying, Go there.

The one who *obeys* God's instruction for today will develop a keen awareness of His direction for tomorrow.

A woman who lives with the stress of an *overwhelmed* schedule will often ache with the sadness of an underwhelmed soul.

Instead of waiting for the time to get started to simply appear one day, we need to be *intentional* with scheduling it.

The *decisions* you make determine the *schedule* you keep. The schedule you keep determines the *life* you live. And how you live your life determines how you spend your *soul*.

Never is a woman so *fulfilled* as when she chooses to underwhelm her schedule so she can let *God* overwhelm her soul.

CHAPTER 4: SOMETIMES I MAKE IT ALL SO COMPLICATED

Knowledge is *wisdom* that comes from acquiring *truth*. *Insight* is wisdom that comes from living out the truth we acquire. *Discernment* is wisdom that comes from the Holy Spirit's reminders of that *knowledge* and *insight*.

1) Have you been reading and praying through God's Word lately?
2) Have you been applying God's Word in your life lately?
3) Have you sought godly counsel and insights from wise people who know specifics about your situation?

Best Yes *answers* are much more likely to happen when we are in the habit of *seeking* wisdom. We have to put our hearts and our minds in places where wisdom gathers, not scatters.

We must be *careful* just simply going with our gut if we haven't checked it against truth-based knowledge and insight.

Never despise the mundane. *Embrace* it. *Unwrap* it like a gift. And be one of the rare few who looks deeper than just the surface. See something more in the everyday. It's there.

Wisdom makes decisions today that will still be good tomorrow.

CHAPTER 5: GOD'S WORD, WAYS, AND WONDER

Delay, unlike sugar, will not always help things go down better.

It's not wrong to use *wisdom*, *knowledge*, and an *understanding* of your resource capacity to assess your decisions.

Do I have the *resources* to handle this request along with my current responsibilities? Could this fit:

* Physically?
* Financially?
* Spiritually?
* Emotionally?

God's Word addresses the approach I take with my activities. God's ways address the attitude I have with my activities. God's wonder is the assurance that not every activity is my activity.

If the activity we're considering is in line with God's Word but our *approach* to that activity isn't, we will overdraw ourselves and bankrupt this part of our lives.

When we *slip* at *living* out the Word of God, we slip at living in the will of God.

God's way is *love*. My way must be a way of love. As I make this *choice*, I must consider what this choice will cost me in my *attitude*. My attitude of love must trump my activity.

Today's *choices* become tomorrow's *circumstances*.

Our decisions aren't just isolated choices. Our decisions *point* our lives in the directions we're about to head. Show me a decision and I'll show you a direction.

What's a decision you are in the midst of making? *Chase* it down. If you do this, where will it most likely *lead?* And then what? And then? Keep going until you walk it all the way out.

We must *understand* all five parts of decision making:

1. *Trusting in God* by placing my desire under His authority.
2. Analyzing the decision.
3. Making the decision.
4. Owning the decision.
5. *Trusting God* to work good even from the not-so-good parts.

If you *desire* to *please* God with the decision you make and afterward it proves to be a mistake, it's an *error* not an *end*.

We *steer* where we *stare*.

When I stare at *failure*, I'll fear it. I'll convince myself it's the worst thing that could happen. And I'll stay stuck.

It's better to *step out* and find out than to *stay stuck*.

There is no *perfect* decision—only the perfectly surrendered decision to press through our fears and know that God is working in us to bring about good through us.

My imperfections will never override *God's promises*. God's promises are not dependent on my ability to always choose well, but rather on His ability to use well.

CHAPTER 8: CONSIDER THE TRADE

If I want to *choose* a Best Yes, it's crucial I make room for it first. Otherwise, a Best Yes can quickly become a stressed yes. And a stressed yes is like snow on a tree that refuses to release its leaves. It causes *cracks* and *breaks* at our core.

If we *refuse* to release before we add, we will get overloaded.

Choices and *consequences* come in package deals. When we make a choice, we ignite the consequences that can come along with it.

Refusing to *release* often means refusing to have *peace*. I trade my peace for a weight of regret. And it's a bad trade.

When we release in peace, we signal we're now ready to *receive*. Receive what's *next*. Receive what's *best*. Receive what's meant for this season, right now.

CHAPTER 9: SHOW UP TO PRACTICE

A Best Yes is a wise yes. And *wisdom* needs to be *practiced* day after day if we are going to know how to apply it to the Best Yes decisions when they come.

If we want to know what to do when it *matters* most, we've got to be *committed* to showing up to practice.

If we aren't walking in *wisdom*, we are walking in *folly*. And folly's ways lead to death.

CHAPTER 10: MANAGING DEMANDS MEANS UNDERSTANDING EXPECTATIONS

Here are some great questions to ask when determining if the *expectations* we're agreeing to with this yes are really realistic or not:

- It feels thrilling to say yes to this now. But how will this yes feel two weeks, two months, and six months from now?

- Do any of the expectations that come from this yes feel forced or frantic?

- Could any part of this yes be tied to people pleasing and allowing that desire to skew my judgment of what's realistic and unrealistic?

- Which wise (older, grounded in God's Word, more experienced, and more mature) people in my life think this is a good idea?

- Are there any facts I try to avoid or hide when discussing this with my wise advisors?

What makes an expectation unrealistic? When an opportunity *stretches* me to a breaking point, it becomes unrealistic. Usually for me the areas I have to consider are:

+ *My time.* The schedule required to meet all the demands of this opportunity isn't in line with the time I have to invest.

+ *My ability.* I'm not equipped with the necessary skills to carry out the functions of this opportunity.

+ *My money.* I can't afford the financial responsibilities that come along with this opportunity.

+ *My passion.* The responsibilities of this opportunity evoke a sense of dread instead of fulfillment in my heart.

+ *My season.* There is something that must take a higher priority during this season of my life, therefore the timing is off for me to take this opportunity.

CHAPTER 11: THE POWER OF THE SMALL NO

A *small no* pushes through the resistance of

awkwardness and disappointment because it's

better to nip something early on.

Delay hardly ever makes a request *go away*. Quite the opposite. It does three things that are unfair to the people waiting for our answer:

- It builds their hopes that our answer will be a yes.
- It prevents them from making other plans.
- It makes an eventual no much harder to receive.

What if a small no can be given in such a way that it becomes a *gift* rather than a *curse*?

If you haven't *carefully* traced out in advance whether you want to go through and to the places that river flows, you'll be in trouble.

Sometimes the greater act of *faith* is to let God lead us, talk to us, and instruct us *beside* the water.

CHAPTER 12: THE AWKWARD
DISAPPOINTMENT OF SAYING NO

It's not a matter of gaining more *confidence*. It's a matter of being more certain of our *convictions*. Confidence is being more certain of our abilities. Conviction is being more certain of God's instructions.

Saying yes all the time won't make me *Wonder Woman*. It will make me a worn-out woman.

I will not let the awkward disappointment of others keep me from my *Best Yes* appointments with God.

Appointment and *disappointment* walk hand in hand. To accept one invitation is to decline another.

CHAPTER 13: BUT WHAT IF I SAY NO AND THEY STOP LIKING ME?

If the person you are trying so hard not to disappoint will be *displeased* by a no, they'll eventually be disappointed even if you say yes.

Unrealistic demands lead to *undercurrents* of failure. So don't allow the unrealistic demands of others to march freely into your life.

Those who constantly try to *impress* others will quickly *depress* themselves.

Saying no isn't an unnecessary *rejection*. It's a necessary *protection* of our Best Yes answers.

We will have a very hard time paying *attention* to those Best Yes answers if we live lives that are completely spent. Instead, why not completely spend yourself on the assignments that are yours, those *moments* you shouldn't dare miss, the *calling* that pulses in your soul, the love you and only you can offer?

CHAPTER 15: THE THRILL OF AN UNRUSHED YES

Relationships *nourish* us in ways nothing else can. It's the relationships that help unrush us.

Do what you need to do to *protect* and *strengthen* the fabric of your relationships. It is okay to get help. Divide up your responsibilities. And if you don't have any way to get help, then reduce your task list. Do what you need to do to have *healthy* relationships.

We do what we *do* and *feel* how we feel because we think what we think.

You know what *pattern* of thought feeds our insecurities most? A fixed mind-set versus a growth mind-set.

We find *security* when we tie our mind-sets to the potential of Jesus' work in us.

People with *growth* mind-sets see their abilities, talents, skills, relationships, and intelligence with potential. Where they are today is a starting place, not a finish line.

Every time I say I am a *child* of *God*, I have to remove the *but* and instead use the word *therefore* to usher God's promise into my reality. We must cut the *but*!

Just as our *bodies* need oxygen, our *souls* need truth flowing steadily in and out.

247

Humility and *wisdom* are a package deal. And often the people who have the most wisdom have experienced the most humility. Or sometimes even the most humiliation.

Wisdom will help us not repeat the *mistakes* we've made but rather grow *stronger* through them.

Together is a really good word. *Together* is what we need when we hit tough patches in life. Making decisions when life is making you cry shouldn't be done alone.

CHAPTER 18: WHEN MY BEST YES
DOESN'T YIELD WHAT I EXPECT

No matter what *wrong* thing has happened, there is a *right* next thing to do.

In the midst of the unexpected, we have the *opportunity* to make one of our greatest Best Yes decisions ever. Let this unexpected happening point to your strength, not your weakness.

It's not the activities or accomplishments we string together that make lives well lived as much as it is the *hearts* of wisdom we gain and use along the way.

Every day we make *choices*. Then our choices make us.

Oh, God, might I be turning that *central* part of me, the part that chooses, into something different than it was before.

Wisdom is either *displayed* or *betrayed* by our actions.

Let's use the two most powerful words, *yes* and *no*, with resounding assurance, graceful clarity, and guided power. All so people may see Jesus when they see us. Hear Jesus when they hear us. And know Jesus when they know us.

Now let's go and live the Best Yes life.

"Chase Down That Decision" Tool

THE DECISIONS WE MAKE TODAY MATTER. EVERY DECISION points us in the direction we are about to travel. No decision is an isolated choice. It's a chain of events. So we've got to get good at chasing down our decisions. We need to look ahead to see where they will take us—and make sure that's really where we want to go. It's wisdom that comes straight from the book of Proverbs:

> A prudent person foresees danger and takes precautions.
> The simpleton goes blindly on and suffers the consequences.
> (22:3 NLT)

To get an idea of what it looks like to apply this principle even in the small decisions of everyday life, read the personal story Lysa shares below. Use the story as a reference for the questions that follow.

CHASING DOWN LATTES

The other day one of my friends asked me if I wanted to try her caramel-crunch-latte-love-something-fancy-with-whip-on-the-top. Yes, please. I would very much like to try that. But I didn't. Why? Because I know myself very well. I won't crave something I never try. But if I try a sugary delish, I will crave said sugary delish. I will not just want a sip. I will want a whole one to myself. And then I will want a whole one to myself several times a week. So, let me chase down this decision.

I found out that drink has 560 calories. If I get in the habit of having three of those per week for the next year and change nothing about my current eating and exercising habits, I will take in an additional 87,360 calories. Thirty-five hundred calories equals one pound of fat. So, give or take how my body chemistry may process all this, according to math alone, I am set to gain about twenty-five pounds during this next year. When I chase down that decision, I refuse sips of drinks like these.

People laugh sometimes when I tell them this little process of mine and say, "Well, you're just a disciplined person." Not really. Did you catch that part about how a sip for me would lead to enjoying this treat three times a week? I'm not really disciplined. I'm just determined—determined not to go places I don't want to go simply because I didn't take time to honestly evaluate. I've felt the heavy weight of regret and I don't want to return there.

I recognize some things happen to us that are beyond our control. But there's a whole lot that happens simply because we don't know how powerful it is to chase down a decision.

In which of the following areas of life do you need to make a decision?

- PHYSICAL: food, exercise, rest, medical care, etc.
- FINANCIAL: earning, giving, saving, spending, debt, margin, etc.
- EMOTIONAL: contentment, healing, peace of mind, etc.
- SPIRITUAL: putting God first, time alone with God, prayer, study, etc.
- RELATIONAL: spouse, kids, extended family, friends, colleagues, neighbors, etc.
- OTHER:

Circle one of the items you checked and use it as a focus for the remainder of this activity.

Using the prompts below, chase down your decision. Write your responses in the designated places on the diagram that follows.

- MY DECISION. Briefly identify a challenge or decision you face in the area of life you circled.
- IDENTIFY POTENTIAL DANGERS. One of the first things Lysa did with her latte decision was to consider the potential dangers—in this case, her self-defeating tendency to crave a sugary delish. What self-defeating tendencies or other potential dangers are you aware of in connection with the situation you identified?

- FACE FACTS. Next, Lysa gathered some facts, specifically, the calorie count of the latte. What are the facts you know or could research about the situation you identified?
- ADD IT UP. Once Lysa had the facts, she chased down her decision by adding them up. Imagine making this same decision over and over. Adding up the cumulative impact of this decision will help you see its compounding effect.
- TAKE PRECAUTIONS. After adding it up, the final step is to take precautions. For Lysa, that meant not taking a sip of her friend's latte. What precautions might you need to take to avoid negative consequences in your decision?
- GET PERSPECTIVE. Now that you see where this decision will take you, answer this question: Is this really where you want to go? If not, back up and change your course by changing your decision.

When you are done with your diagram on the next page, ask God for the additional guidance or strength you need in order to take the next step with your decision.

For a printable pdf of this diagram, please
visit www.TheBestYes.com.

Notes

Chapter 3: Overwhelmed Schedule, Underwhelmed Soul

1. Joseph Durso, "Fearless Fosbury Flops to Glory," *New York Times*, October 20, 1968, http://www.nytimes.com/packages/html/sports /year_in_sports/10.20.html.

Chapter 4: Sometimes I Make It All So Complicated

1. *Merriam Webster's Collegiate Dictionary*, 11th ed., s.v. "intuition."

Chapter 5: God's Word, Ways, and Wonder

1. Oswald Chambers, "Learning About His Ways," *My Utmost for His Highest*, August 1, 2012, http://utmost.org/learning-about-his-ways/.

Chapter 6: Chase Down That Decision

1. Andy Stanley, *The Principle of the Path* (Nashville: Thomas Nelson, 2008), 15.
2. Ibid., 39–40.

Chapter 7: Analysis Paralysis

1. David Kinnaman, *You Lost Me* (Grand Rapids: Baker Books, 2011), 100–101.

Chapter 10: Managing Demands Means Understanding Expectations

1. Lysa TerKeurst, *What Happens When Women Say Yes to God Devotional* (Eugene, OR: Harvest House Publishers, 2013), 131–134.

Chapter 11: The Power of the Small No

1. Christa, June 5, 2013 (1:26 p.m.), comment on Lysa TerKeurst, "Why

Do We Have Such a Hard Time Saying 'No?' " *Lysa TerKeurst* (blog), June 5, 2013, http://lysaterkeurst.com/2013/06 /why-do-we-have-such-a-hard-time-saying-no/.

2. Connie, June 5, 2013 (2:55 p.m.), comment on Lysa TerKeurst, "Why Do We Have Such a Hard Time Saying 'No?'" *Lysa TerKeurst* (blog), June 5, 2013, http://lysaterkeurst.com/2013/06/why-do-we-have-such-a-hard-time-saying-no/.

3. Brené Brown, Ph.D., LMSW, is a research professor at the University of Houston Graduate College of Social Work. This quotation is from *Daring Greatly* (New York: Penguin, 2012), PDF e-book, chapter 6.

Chapter 12: The Awkward Disappointment of Saying No

1. Tina, June 5, 2013 (1:22 p.m.), comment on Lysa TerKeurst, "Why Do We Have Such a Hard Time Saying 'No?'" *Lysa TerKeurst* (blog), June 5, 2013, http://lysaterkeurst.com/2013/06/why-do-we-have-such-a-hard-time-saying-no/.

2. Jeanne, June 5, 2013 (1:21 p.m.), comment on Lysa TerKeurst, "Why Do We Have Such a Hard Time Saying 'No?'" *Lysa TerKeurst* (blog), June 5, 2013, http://lysaterkeurst.com/2013/06/why-do-we-have-such-a-hard-time-saying-no/.

3. Jane, June 5, 2013 (3:01 p.m.), comment on Lysa TerKeurst, "Why Do We Have Such a Hard Time Saying 'No?'" *Lysa TerKeurst* (blog), June 5, 2013, http://lysaterkeurst.com/2013/06 /why-do-we-have-such-a-hard-time-saying-no/.

Chapter 13: But What If I Say No and They Stop Liking Me?

1. *Life Application Study Bible–NIV* (Grand Rapids: Zondervan, 1984), 735.

2. Matthew Henry, "2 Chronicles 16," *Concise Commentary on the Whole Bible, Bible Hub,* http://biblehub.com/commentaries/mhc/2 _chronicles/16.htm.

3. Lori, June 5, 2013 (1:33 p.m.), comment on Lysa TerKeurst, "Why Do We Have Such a Hard Time Saying 'No?'" *Lysa TerKeurst* (blog), June 5, 2013, http://lysaterkeurst.com/2013/06/why-do-we-have-such-a-hard-time-saying-no/.

Chapter 14: A Best Yes Is Seen by Those Who Choose to See

1. Bob Goff, *Love Does* (Nashville: Thomas Nelson, 2012), 9.
2. Ibid., 216.
3. Ida Minerva Tarbell and John McCan Davis, *The Early Life of Abraham Lincoln* (New York: S. S. McClure, 1898), 235.

Chapter 15: The Thrill of an Unrushed Yes

1. Erik Qualman, *Digital Leader* (New York: McGraw Hill, 2012): quoted in David Murray, "10 Digital Commandments," *HeadHeartHand Blog*, February 9, 2012, http://headhearthand.org /blog/2012/02/09/10-digital-commandments/.
2. Lysa TerKeurst, *What Happens When Women Say Yes to God Devotional* (Eugene, OR: Harvest House Publishers, 2013), 127–130.

Chapter 16: The Panic That Keeps You from Your Best Yes

1. BC Lifesaving Society (2000): quoted in Joel Sutcliffe, "Drowning Physiology," NLS Course Pack, 2003, http://www.sutcliffe.ca/joel /nls/drowning.pdf.
2. Comment on my Facebook page from Kathy White Hall.
3. Carol Dweck, "What is Mindset," *Mindset*, 2006–2010, http:// mindsetonline.com/whatisit/about/.
4. Carol Dweck, "The Nature of Change," *Mindset*, 2006–2010, http:// mindsetonline.com/changeyourmindset/natureofchange/.

Chapter 18: When My Best Yes Doesn't Yield What I Expect

1. "Roosevelt's Pocket Diary (Memory)," *American Treasures of the Library of Congress*, July 27, 2010, http://www.loc.gov/exhibits /treasures/trm052.html.
2. "Theodore Roosevelt—Biographical," *Nobelprize.org*, 2013, http:// www.nobelprize.org/nobel_prizes/peace/laureates/1906/ roosevelt-bio.html.

Chapter 19: We Make Choices. Then Our Choices Make Us.

1. C. S. Lewis, *Mere Christianity* (New York: HarperCollins, 1952), 93.

Scripture Index

About the Author

LYSA TERKEURST IS A WIFE TO ART AND MOM TO FIVE priority blessings named Jackson, Mark, Hope, Ashley, and Brooke. She is the president of Proverbs 31 Ministries and author of seventeen books, including the *New York Times* bestsellers *Unglued* and *Made to Crave*. Additionally, Lysa has been featured on *Focus on the Family*, *The Today Show*, *Good Morning America*, and more. Lysa speaks nationwide at Catalyst, Women of Faith, and various church events.

To those who know her best, Lysa is simply a carpooling mom who loves Jesus passionately, is dedicated to her family, and struggles like the rest of us with laundry, junk drawers, and cellulite.

ᪿ

WEBSITE: If you enjoyed *The Best Yes*, equip yourself with additional resources at www.TheBestYes.com, www.LysaTerKeurst.com, and www.Proverbs31.org.

SOCIAL MEDIA: Connect with Lysa on a daily basis, see pictures of her family, and follow her speaking schedule:

- BLOG: www.LysaTerKeurst.com
- FACEBOOK: www.Facebook.com/OfficialLysa
- INSTAGRAM: @LysaTerKeurst
- TWITTER: @LysaTerKeurst